ACCOUNTING FOR AUTHORS

D.F. HART &
MARK LESLIE LEFEBVRE

Stark Publishing Solutions

Stark Publishing Solutions
An Imprint of Stark Publishing
Waterloo, Ontario
www.starkpublishing.ca

Publisher's Note: This work is derived from the real-world experience of the authors to offer insights, how-to, and recommend best practices with it comes to accounting and the business of writing in general. It does not constitute legal or tax advice. The publisher and authors strongly recommend you seek legal and taxation advice from professionals local to and familiar with your region's tax laws.

Accounting for Authors / D.F. Hart & Mark Leslie Lefebvre
April 2022

Print ISBN: 978-1-989351-67-3
eBook ISBN: 978-1-989351-68-0

Dedication

*To my fellow authors — You are awesome, unique, magical
wordsmithing warriors. Stay the course, it's worth it.*

D.F. Hart

*For Peter Duffus — For helping me face Math head on when
it frightened me the most. And for nurturing my creative
spirit via inspiring talks and a life changing LDHS marketing
assignment that leveraged my storytelling passion.*

*And for Mom — Who managed the modest finances of our
single-income blue collar family in a way that made us all feel
rich inside and out.*

Mark Leslie Lefebvre

Table of Contents

A NOTE ON AUTHORSHIP, VOICE, AND RESOURCES

While this is a co-authored book, the authors preserved their distinct voices rather than attempt to blend the narrative into a single perspective.

Thus, each of the chapter and some sub-chapters will include a denotation of either **DFH** (for D.F. Hart) or **MLL** (for Mark Leslie Lefebvre) to indicate the perspective and voice used for that segment.

In addition, while resources are mentioned and links are offered throughout this book, all hyperlinks, downloadable resources, and the tables/graphs/charts shared can be found at the following site:

www.starkpublishing.ca/accounting

FOREWORD

MLL

There are two things that are important for you to know about me and how it led to deciding to co-author this book with D.F. Hart.

First, I have an unwavering conviction that regardless of the journey you are on—traditional publishing, self-publishing, or some combination of the two—being an author is a business.

Second, I have never been good at finances, have had to dig myself out of debt numerous times, and when I was young, I constantly struggled with math.

Why are those two things the insights I'm leading with to open this book?

The first one is, I hope, obvious.

For most of my adult life as a representative in the bookselling industry, and as an author coach and mentor, much of the work I've done has involved helping authors understand and embrace the business aspects of being a writer. My *Stark Reflections on Writing & Publishing* podcast, and the *Stark Publishing Solutions* series this book is a part of, have that as a central focus.

The second one might be a little more confusing.

Why would I share that I've struggled with debt, finances, and math in the foreword of a book entitled *Accounting for Authors*?

It's to help you understand that if someone like me can decide to look directly into the terrifying and frustrating faces of topics like accounting, finances, and math, complete with the nebulous history of our tumultuous relationship, then you can too.

I have worked in the book industry since 1992. It was a landmark year for me, simultaneously becoming a bookseller and having my very first short story appear in print after years of writing and a multitude of rejections.

Over the decades, which included managing at brick-and-mortar and online bookstores, running a print on demand business (the Espresso Book Machine at the bookstore at McMaster University), and establishing a self-publishing platform (Kobo Writing Life), I learned a lot about the business of selling books in all its formats (print, eBook, and audiobook).

But not a single day goes by where I don't continue to learn even more about the business. I learn from a combination of first-hand experience, reading books and articles, listening to podcasts, and interacting with industry people and other authors.

Even when I'm working with new writers, answering their questions, and helping them come up with their own unique strategies and approaches to writing and publishing, I'm also learning.

I'm taking those learnings and applying them to my author business, but also sharing them with those looking for help and support.

It's a process, a journey, an ongoing evolving experience.

My relationship with math, finances, and accounting—despite my inherent fear of them—is no different.

The only subject I consistently did well in was English. Science and Math were difficult for me. Math, in particular, threw me for a loop.

When I was in grade 12 (these were back in the days in Ontario, Canada, when high school was five years, and went up to grade 13), Pete Duffus, our high school's guidance counselor got me involved in tutoring younger math students at the 9th and 10th grade levels.

"But I struggle with math," I said, not understanding his logic. "Don't you want these students to learn from someone getting straight As in math instead of someone who has to work hard just to get a C minus?"

"You'll be able to help them," he told me, "Because you can understand why and where they're having difficulty."

And he was right. When one of the younger students I was tutoring in math was staring down a problem, I could clearly see the roadblock from their perspective. So, instead of showing them the answer, I worked through the problem *with* them.

That process, and experience, not only helped my tutees raise their scores on tests, but my own grades, similarly, improved. I didn't become an A student, but moving from a C- to a B was a solid win for me.

My mother knew how I struggled with managing money. If I had a dollar in my pocket, it was destined to be spent. It was the classic case of *a fool and his money are soon parted*.

So, when I went off to university, she advised me to track where my money was going, beginning the process of helping me understand a budget.

I took a cardstock folder (what we, in Canada refer to as a duotang, based on the brand name Duo-Tang™) gave it the title *Money Matters* (note my cheeky play on words), and, on lined paper, broke it into **Income** and **Expenses**. Under **Expenses**, I further divided little quadrants into *Living*, *School*, and *Entertainment*.

Just tracking where my money was going didn't immediately make me better at budgeting. But it was a first solid step in understanding where the money was coming from (a combination of student loans, parental generosity, and part-time employment), and where it was going.

The "where it was going" part was fascinating because there were items that were not under my control. Monthly rent and utilities were fixed. School supplies, such as textbooks were mostly fixed with some potential bartering (used textbooks, leveraging library resources, and creative swaps with fellow students). But what I spent on food, clothing, and personal entertainment was almost entirely within my control.

That's when I learned that accounting, and finances, and balancing a budget weren't all about hard, fast, and cold numbers. It could involve creativity. And it could involve tough decisions.

This may seem silly, but one of the first challenges I faced involved a food condiment. I'd always been a Heinz® ketchup guy. No exceptions. But the cost of the brand I loved compared to the no-name brand was one dollar more. I ended up finding that extra dollar by sacrificing it from a different part of my budget. (In case it's not obvious, the parallel here is that sometimes, to work with a better editor, one who costs more, because of the higher quality of the work that person does, you'll have to figure out what other part of your author expenditures you can take those extra funds from).

And thus, finances, budgeting, and accounting could be, like the fictional plots I was weaving, creative, and fun.

Over the years, I've continued to make mistakes and plenty of poor decisions along the way. I've miscalculated things or planned poorly based on a faulty forecast. And I've dipped in and out of debt.

But the fundamental tracking of income and expenses has ensured the most important baselines. I can easily see where and how things went wrong. And understanding and seeing those numbers in stark detail is an excellent first step in being able to make those adjustments.

To this day, I continue to track my income and expenses and leverage the power of spreadsheet formulas to help ensure I'm putting away a specific percent to pay income taxes to the provincial and federal Canadian governments.

I am a lot more organized and stricter about tracking, saving, and filing receipts, not only because it's my entire livelihood, but I've been doing this now for decades.

Because writing is a business.

And understanding the fundamentals of accounting, and tracking, and budgeting are a critical part of any business.

I'm still not all that good with math, or finances, but I keep working at it, and keep trying to become better with discovering the right balance that works for me.

When D.F. approached me with the idea of co-authoring this book, I had nearly the same response as I did back in high school, when my guidance counsellor suggested I do math tutoring.

"But I struggle with accounting," the words were almost out of my lips before I stopped myself in an odd déjà vu moment.

I pondered this.

D.F. has an MBA and has worked in accounting for over twenty-five years. When I first interviewed her for my podcast, I was impressed and inspired by just how detailed she tracked every single cost related to publishing and marketing her books.

Her background, skills, and decades of experience make her ideal for a book like this.

So, where then do I come in?

I, perhaps like you, still have plenty to learn. Accounting, budgeting, managing the financial aspects of my author business is an ongoing exercise. Not all that different, when you think about it, to the things I continue to learn about the business of writing and publishing.

So, as a co-author, one of my main tasks is ensuring that the details, explanations, examples, and instructional materials that D.F. crafts are simple, easy to understand, and clear—even to a novice like myself.

And, where applicable, to insert my own decades of experience as an author as well as a book industry representative, to flesh out some of the fundamentals of the business of this industry.

Collaborating on this book with D.F. has helped me improve upon and better understand some of the basics of accounting that are so critical to establishing and maintaining a successful author business.

I'm positive that it, dear reader, can help you too.

And one last thing.

If you're like me, and still find accounting terminology and methods a bit intimidating, you may notice me step in occasionally—in the same way I did when I was tutoring other students in math—and confirm that we'll get through this together. After all, in D.F., we not only have a patient and expert teacher, but someone who understands being an author **and** an accountant, and who wants to help and support us on our own journeys.

And we couldn't ask for anyone better to do this for us.

INTRODUCTION

DFH

If I had to guess, I would say that you have picked up this book for one of two reasons:

- Possibility #1 – You want your author business to have as solid a foundation as you can make it.

- Possibility #2—You are morbidly curious, thinking: *"Accounting for Authors"? Seriously? What could accounting possibly have to do with me writing books?*

The short answer? *More than you might realize.*

And this book will walk you through the 'why', then show you the 'how,' so that you can interpret all the data that comes at us as authors: number of sales, downloads of a free book, promo spend results—all of it, including most important figure of all—*how much profit have I made?*

I am going to walk you through some accounting and finance principles and concepts, using real-life examples and every-day language, so that you can more efficiently manage (and hopefully grow) your *author business.*

Because a business is exactly what this is. The moment you assigned your 'book baby' a price tag and put it up for sale, you became a published author—and if you independently published your book, you also became a *business owner.*

Now, I realize that some people do not like numbers and do not like math (confession: *I* do not like math very much, either!) and there's a good chance that those people reading this right now have just laid their head down on the closest hard, flat surface and are banging it lightly.

But D.F. [thunk] *I do not **want** [thunk] to do numbers and math stuff* [thunk]...*I just wanna **write**!*

I get that, and I feel you. I do. But trust me when I say that the health of your business is going to be better served if you at least understand the basics.

Now, having said that, let me get two disclaimers out into the great wide open before we delve too far into things.

1) I am NOT a CPA (and do not want to be one.) I am also NOT a tax professional or a lawyer (and do not want to be one). **You should address tax and business structure-related questions and concerns with a qualified professional.**

And here's why: Knowledge of accounting does *not* automatically equal tax knowledge.

Think of it like this - We would not expect a calculus professor to be able to step in and teach a 14th century Italian Literature class. Just because each course is led by a certified teacher does not mean that each teacher is fluent in every single course that is offered on campus. We would also not schedule heart surgery with a podiatrist, even though the podiatrist is also a doctor and went to medical school just like the thoracic surgeon did.

Similarly, it simply cannot be presumed that everyone with an accounting background can adequately – and correctly - address *all* your business and tax questions.

The entire realm of tax is complicated, ever-changing, and varies not just from country to country but even from state to state within the US. So, *you really do need to find someone whose <u>specialty</u> is navigating that topic.*

2) Nor will I be offering financial or other advice re-garding 'should I do audiobooks or not,' etcetera. **Those types of decisions need to happen as part of your own personal approach to being an author and what your goals are.**

But what I *can* (and will happily) do is show you the basics of accounting, and some finance concepts, and how to apply them and hopefully, increase both your knowledge base *and* your comfort level if numbers are not your favorite thing.

And once you learn these concepts, you can rest easy, because unlike other author-related topics, there are two cool things about accounting that you may or may not know:

1) **It is evergreen.** The concepts I am going to share with you have not changed and will not change. At all. (Unless we are all overrun by aliens or

something, in which case, we all will have bigger problems to worry about!)

2) **Accounting concepts are universal.** By this I mean, it does not matter if you are in the United States or in Europe or in Australia or wherever. These concepts will be applicable *regardless* of location, currency, the number of books you have out—or even what structure you decide on for your business. It also doesn't matter if you are Amazon exclusive, or a 'wide' author, or traditionally published, or a combination of these things. The concepts in this book will still apply!

The main goal of this book is to achieve the "Three E's":
1) Easy to follow
2) Educational
3) Entertaining

(Because let's face it, for a lot of folks, accounting and finance topics are the emotional equivalent of "Bueller.... Bueller...")

Okay, take a breath, grab something to drink, and get comfortable.

Are you ready?

Good. I am too. Let's get started, shall we?

CHAPTER ONE:
Business Structure Type

DFH

Before we cover the basics of business structures, I need you to stop and seriously think about one vital question:

What's your "why"?

By that I mean: *Why are you an author? What are your end goals*—and, in tandem: *What's your definition of 'success'?*

Is it to produce books to give to family and friends?

Is it make a part-time living?

A full-time living?

There's no 'one right answer' here; it will vary for you and any other person reading this. Not only that, but over time, you may find that your 'why' has changed. And that's okay.

But these are questions you need to know the answers to—because your answers can (and should) impact your next set of decisions.

And the next set. And the set after that.

For example, if you embrace authorship as a beloved hobby, there's no need to select a more complex business structure. If you plan to write part-time or full-time, however, you may eventually want—or need—to 'trade up' from the initial level you choose to something that offers you more personal liability protections.

So—answer the *'what's your why'* questions first. Establish those foundational parameters for yourselves, dear readers, and *then* keep reading.

***

Now that you've got your answers about your *why*, one of the first things you need to decide is under what type of setup your business will operate.

Here in the United States, most authors will opt for one of the three more popular types listed below, as defined by the Internal Revenue Service and the Small Business Administration:

<u>Sole Proprietorship</u>: This is a single-owner setup and is the easiest (and cheapest) to establish, and a separate taxpayer ID number for the business is not a requirement. The single biggest drawback to the sole proprietor setup is that if something goes wrong (a lawsuit, for example), your <u>personal</u> assets (your house, your car, your personal bank accounts) can be at risk, because there is *no degree of separation between you and the business.*

<u>Limited Liability Company (LLC)</u>: This setup can be a single owner or multiple people, and it can include members that live outside the United States. An LLC protects your personal assets in the event something goes wrong. You do not have to pay corporate taxes, but LLC members "are considered self-employed and must pay self-employment tax contributions toward Medicare and

Social Security" (https://www.sba.gov/business-guide/launch-your-business/choose-business-structure).

Corporation (INC): There are four types of corporation setups in the United States, with the C-corporation being the most recognizable to most people. Corporations are the most expensive route to take regarding setup costs, and while the owners are even more insulated from their personal assets being at risk if something goes wrong, unlike LLC's and sole proprietorships, corporations must pay income taxes on their profits.

To learn more about these and other business structures in the United States, I *strongly recommend* visiting the US Small Business Administration's website at https://www.sba.gov/.

But because certain requirements can vary by state, I *also* recommend talking to a CPA or other qualified professional *in your local area* that can explain the pros and cons of each business type and help you figure out which path is optimal for you.

If you live outside the United States, I *strongly recommend* communicating with your area's governing body to find out which business structure in your country makes the most sense for you. Some resource links are provided below to assist you!

Australia
https://asic.gov.au/

Canada

https://www.canada.ca/en/revenue-agency

European Union

https://ec.europa.eu/info/business-economy-euro/doing-business-eu

New Zealand

https://www.business.govt.nz/starting-a-business/

United Kingdom

https://www.gov.uk/topic/company-registration-filing

CHAPTER TWO:
What's up With the Weird Words?

DFH

I think some of the mystique around accounting and finance stems in part from industry terms that often just do not translate well to plain English. To be fair, it is *not* the only arena full of amazingly—and overly—complicated descriptions (I'm looking at *you*, tax codes, and every single math textbook I've ever encountered).

Yet accounting concepts underpin a chunk of what we do in our daily lives, although we often do not realize it. (And yes, I will mention specific examples here shortly).

So, how do authors learn these things—*without* the five-dollar words or mile-long definitions?

That is where this book comes in.

Below is a list of accounting and finance concepts and terms that will be *most applicable* in the author world, no matter where you live, what kind of business structure or publication path you chose, or how many books you have published (or plan to).

- Risk Tolerance
- Risk Capacity
- Cash-Basis Method
- Accrual-Basis Method
- Double-Entry
- Balance Sheet
- Income Statement

- Revenue
- Assets, Liabilities, and Equity
- Payables and Receivables
- Cost of Sales - aka Cost of Goods Sold (COGS)
- General & Administrative (G&A)—aka Operating or Overhead Expenses
- Break-Even Point
- Gross Income (aka Gross Profit / Loss)
- Net Income (aka Net Profit / Loss)
- Margin
- Net Return
- Return on Investment (ROI)
- Payback Period

Now, over the next several chapters, we'll review these terms within linked batches or groupings so that you can see what they are and how they relate to one another.

But the ones I want to address right now and get out of the way are *risk tolerance, risk capacity, cash-basis, accrual- basis, and double entry.*

***

Risk Tolerance and Risk Capacity

While these two terms are more commonly used and seen in the wealth management and financial services sector, I think they are important for *all* business owners to know, understand, and remember.

Risk Tolerance, in a nutshell, is the amount of uncertainty (or risk) that you as a business owner are comfortable with.

Risk Capacity is the amount of risk that you *must* take to reach your goals.

How do these last two terms relate to being an author?

Well, let's talk about my first audiobook as an example.

Was I comfortable making that investment? Yes, at the time I considered audiobook costs to be within my *risk tolerance level.*

Was that a risk that I absolutely HAD to take at that point in my career for me to be successful?

No. It wasn't. For me personally, doing an audiobook so early in my author journey was a living, breathing example of *overestimating my risk capacity.*

***

Cash-Basis, Accrual-Basis, and Double Entry

Keeping the books for a business can happen one of two ways—either using the **cash-basis method** or the **accrual-basis method**.

In the **cash-basis method**, *items are not recorded until money changes hands.*

In the **accrual-basis method**, *transactions are recorded when they happen, regardless of when the money changes hands.*

Regardless of whether you use the cash-basis or accrual-basis method, all accounting transactions are done via the **double-entry** process. For every entry into expenses, there's a corresponding entry to either your cash account or a holding account, depending on the recording method you are using. And for every sale, there's a corresponding entry to either your cash account (or a holding account) as well.

Think of each transaction as a see-saw—you cannot record only one side, or the see-saw is not balanced. *For everything recorded, there **must** be a balancing of that seesaw.*

***

TAKE A DEEP BREATH

MLL

If you got to the end of this chapter feeling a bit overwhelmed with that list of terms, please don't panic.

I know exactly where you're coming from; because I felt it too the first time I read through this section. Please don't worry or panic. They will make more sense in the forthcoming examples. They'll also appear in the online resources at:

www.starkpublishing.ca/accounting

It's okay if, the first time you read this book, only one or two things stick. We can't expect ourselves to become MBAs like D.F. is overnight. It takes time and practice. Okay, to be completely honest, we can't expect ourselves to become MBAs at all just by reading this book. But we can benefit from reading what D.F. is sharing and absorb at least a couple of new things we can incorporate into our author business lives.

So far, one thing I got out of this chapter is understanding that I've long used the cash-basis method for my own writing business tracking. It just makes sense and is easier for me.

I now understand what she means by the accrual and double-entry process. It was a bit of a flash-back for me to a high school accounting course.

Also, given my personal circumstances, I'm thinking I might stick with my cash-basis tracking method. It works for me.

So don't feel pressured. Use these insights from D.F. to make informed decisions that work for **you**.

For now, take a deep breath. In the next chapter, D.F. is going to introduce a few new terms to the equation (no pun intended) which will help to bring it all together for us as we keep reading.

Okay, now take another deep breath.

You've got this.

CHAPTER THREE:
The Accounting Equation

DFH

Assets, Liabilities and Equity—The Building Blocks of the Accounting Equation

Assets are *the things your business OWNS that have value*. They can be *tangible* (in physical form) or *intangible* (not in physical form).

Tangible assets are things like a building, the money in your bank account and the computer you use to create your stories—*anything that is in physical form and can convert to cash quickly*. For any paperback books you just stocked up on for an upcoming signing event, whether they are considered 'inventory' (tangible asset) or simply expensed depends on whether you are using the accrual-basis method or the cash-basis method.

And I must note that there *is* one weird exception to the 'in physical form' rule.

One tangible asset that every one of us authors have, at this very moment, would be outstanding book royalties that have not yet hit our bank accounts. Monies owed to us like this are classed as '**Accounts Receivables**' in the accrual-basis method. Now, you would think that since they are technically not in 'physical form' that receivables would fall under *intangible*, but surprisingly, since they are considered 'cash or cash equivalent', they do not!

Intangible assets are things like copyrights, patents, trademarks, logos, slogans, and company names.

Some SUPER IMPORTANT NOTES about IP

Intellectual Property (IP) is an asset that every author has, and at its base, is defined as "a work or invention that is the result of creativity." While your Intellectual Property is itself considered to be *intangible,* if you print a copy of your manuscript (for example, a paperback book) that physical copy would be considered a *tangible* asset. If you're in the US, *all* assets are required to be recorded *at cost, not value* — in other words, that copyright of your work needs to hit your books at the cost it *took to acquire it, NOT its potential earnings value.*

***

Liabilities are, quite simply, *the things that your business OWES.*

The most common examples in the author world would be cover design costs, editing/formatting costs, copyright application fees, printing and shipping costs, narration costs, and so forth. These outbound things that you owe are **'Payables.'** There are other things that fall into the liabilities category, but most of them will not apply to most authors' businesses, so I will not bog you down with them here.

***

Equity (sometimes also referred to as **Capital**) is quite simply *what your business has left after everything your business OWES has been paid for*.

***

The Accounting Equation - Demystified

The *accounting equation* is very simple-looking, given that it is one of the fundamental cornerstones of accounting.

Here it is:

Assets = Liabilities + Equity

(Wow, that's great, D.F., but what does that mean?)

So glad you asked. Remember a couple of pages ago when I talked about assets, liabilities, and equity?

Here they are again, in plain language:

Assets—Things your business OWNS.
Liabilities—Things your business OWES.
Equity—What is left over after the things your business OWES are paid for.

Now, look again at that original Accounting Equation:

Assets = Liabilities + Equity

But this time, plug in the simpler definitions.

What is OWNED = What is OWED + What is left

So now, that Accounting Equation becomes less intim-idating, right?

But even in its improved current state, it is still not that helpful for us.

What if we move it around a bit and isolate the part we need? Because if we are being honest, what we are really the most interested in is the 'what's left over' part, right?

Yeppers. So, we spin the equation:

What is left = What is OWNED - what is OWED

Now we are getting somewhere.

And you might not realize it, but I will bet you are already using the Accounting Equation somewhere in your day-to-day activities.

For example:

- Available balance in your checking account = Current bank balance minus any checks you wrote that have not cleared yet

- Take-home pay from a job = The pay you earned minus taxes taken out

- Book Royalty = The selling price of your book minus the storefront's percentage.

Surprise!

Each one of these examples uses that rearranged Accounting Equation!

Pretty cool, huh?

SEE, THAT WASN'T SO BAD

MLL

Aren't you glad you took a deep breath? Isn't it helpful that our master instructor translated that accounting-speak into something that makes sense in our real-world experience?

Those terms from Chapter Two are now applying to things we, as authors, know about. You'll get more as you read on.

CHAPTER FOUR:
Costs: Direct, Indirect, Fixed and Variable

DFH

Cost of Sales (aka Cost of Goods Sold) versus General & Administrative (aka Operating or Overhead Expenses)

These two terms are similar only in that they are both cost (i.e., expense, or **Payable**) categories. Here is what each term means.

Cost of Sales / Cost of Goods Sold are *the expenses that happen as a <u>direct result</u> of production.*

No production means no "Cost of Sales" —*it is directly dependent upon whether you make any product*—or in our world, publish.

General & Administrative / Operating / Overhead Expenses, however, are ever present, whether you publish five hundred books or zero. Your business will incur these expenses no matter what; these are completely independent of production. These are the things that you sometimes hear people refer to as *'the CDB's'*—the 'costs of doing business.'

***

We've just touched briefly on the idea of "overhead" expenses versus "production" costs. Let's dig a little deeper into these two concepts.

Overhead expenses are things like your membership fee to a professional organization, your website domain fees, the fees you pay for your newsletter email service, and so forth. These are also referred to as *indirect costs*.

Regarding **production costs** in the author world, what is 'produced' is our books. So, this is the bucket that cover design, editing and formatting, and all the other expenses that tie back to publishing one of your wonderful stories for folks to enjoy falls into. These are also referred to as *direct costs*.

COGS (Cost of Goods Sold) is the category that your *production costs* land in on your Income Statement. Your *overhead expenses* are usually listed separately on your Income Statement. (The reason for this will become clear when we dive into Gross Profit versus Net Profit / Loss later).

Besides being classed as *overhead* (indirect) or *production* (direct), costs have another distinct characteristic, which is that costs are either **fixed** or **variable**. This characteristic has nothing at all to do with whether a cost is direct or indirect.

Fixed costs are simply that—they stay constant, no matter what's going on, and no matter how many units of something are produced.

In the author world, a fixed cost example in production is cover design—typically, we pay a one-time flat rate per cover.

A good 'overhead' fixed expense example is the annual membership to an author organization.

Variable costs change, and they are typically driven by usage or volume; the more units of something that are produced, the higher your variable costs.

A good example of a variable production cost for authors is selling a paperback book. For each book that is sold, you incur another set of printing and shipping costs.

An excellent example of a variable 'overhead' expense is marketing: namely, cost-per-click ads.

In summary:

- Direct costs = production costs
- Indirect costs = overhead expenses
- Fixed costs = remain constant no matter how much is produced
- Variable costs = changes depending on amount of production

So, here are some concrete examples of how all this lines out in the author realm:

- Cost-per-click Ads—are a variable indirect expense
- Membership Dues—are a fixed indirect expense
- Cover design—is a fixed direct cost

- Shipping costs for paperbacks—is a variable direct cost

Most of us will only look at our direct costs when trying to figure out if we're making a profit on our books. But to truly lock in your actual profit or loss, you really need to include your indirect (overhead) expenses, as well. This is done through what is called cost allocation.

Cost allocation, in simple terms, means that *you spread out the expenses that are not dependent on production (your indirect expenses) across all items produced*.

A good example would be an annual membership fee. Let's say I spend $119 USD per year to be a member of ALLi. To allocate that cost out among my books, I would DIVIDE that expense by the number of titles I have published.

$119 / 16 titles currently = $7.44 per title I would allocate across my catalogue

I have twelve more books planned. So, when I get them published, my allocation of that ALLi membership fee will be less *per book*:

$119 / 28 titles = $4.25 per title

Including your indirect expenses in this manner gives you a much better (and quite frankly, more accurate!) view of where your **break-even point** is; that is, the point past which your sales have covered ALL your expenses, not just production costs, and your business is running at a profit.

Come with me to the next chapter, and let's start to apply what we've learned so far.

HOW ARE YOU HOLDING OUT?

MLL

Admittedly, in this chapter, we got into a slightly deeper dive when talking about the various types of costs. But just a reminder that D.F. used real-life author examples to help them make sense.

A few personal examples (as it never hurts to see further examples of the application of the terms we just covered) that I've taken from this chapter are below.

A few of my own fixed costs include the rate I pay my main cover designer for a single book and the annual charge for Microsoft 365®.

Variable costs would be the costs I pay an editor (as it's based on word count) and the costs for producing a print book (as it's based on page count).

Speaking of print books, whenever I purchase author copies of my own books for re-selling, I allocate the cost of shipping across the costs of those books.

For example, the unit cost for me to order copies of my novel **A Canadian Werewolf in New York** is currently set at $5.62 USD. That is a set or fixed cost.

But the shipping cost, which is variable, depending on the "to" and "from" shipping locations, as well as the weight of the shipment, is an additional cost that I must allocate to the books in a particular order I have placed.

So, in this example, let's say I order 10 copies.

$$\$5.62 \times 10 = \$56.20$$

But the shipping of these books comes to $21.50.

This means I need to add the allocated shipping costs to the production cost of each unit.

$$\$21.50 \div 10 = \$2.15$$

Therefore, the actual, or total cost of each book is really the production cost plus allocated shipping cost.

Production Cost + Allocated Shipping Cost = Total Cost
$5.62 + $2.15 = $7.77

It might be useful for you to pause and do some of your own quick calculations to get a feel for these terms with something concrete and specific to you.

For me, that always helps.

Then we can move on to better understand this concept but with many allocations and variables, and how what we just learned relates to profit, which D.F. covers in the next chapter.

CHAPTER FIVE:
Profits & Other Metrics, Part 1

DFH

Revenue-related Calculations

Let's get started by looking at a real-life example of one of my books and digging into what my costs were to publish it, including allocating out my indirect costs. Then, we will learn how to find the *break-even point* in this chapter, and the *gross income*, the *net income*, and the *gross and net margins* in Chapter Six.

First, I need to list out all my fixed costs associated with publishing *List of Secrets*. The below is what I spent **to get that first unit produced, or in our world, published**.

My fixed direct costs were:

- eBook Cover Design: $200 (2 different covers over time)
- Paperback & LP Covers: $200 ($100 each)
- eBook formatting: $0 (I did it myself)
- Paperback formatting: $200
- Editing / Proofreading: $900 (will split this out across the three formats)

- ISBN number: $5.75 x 3 (I bought a block of 100 for $575, so $5.75 each per format)*

*(**Note:** *while eBooks do not require an ISBN, I opt to assign one to each of my eBooks to maintain control as the publisher on record.*)

Total **fixed direct** for <u>ALL formats</u> combined: $1,517.25

Total **fixed direct** *per format* came out to:
eBook = $505.75
Paperback = $405.75
Large Print = $605.75

And here are my **fixed indirect expenses** allocated against this title:

- ALLI Membership Fee: $7.44
- Mailchimp: $57.51
- Bookfunnel: $11.88
- Microsoft: $11.58
- ScribeCount: $4.38
- StoryOrigin: $4.66
- Wordpress: $21.11
- WooCommerce: $1.96
- GSuite: $4.87

Total **fixed indirect** expenses allocated to this title:
$125.39

***

Break-Even Point

Basically, **break-even point** is the "sweet spot"—the point that you have sold enough of your product to completely recoup your costs. Any sales beyond your break-even point are purely profit.

The formula to calculate break-even units sold is:
Break-Even Units = Total <u>Fixed</u> Costs / (Price per Unit - <u>Variable</u> Cost per Unit)

List of Secrets is book number two in my mystery and thriller series. It is available in eBook, paperback, and large print paperback formats.

For the purposes of calculating break-even point BY TITLE, we should ideally include ALL costs incurred, regardless of format type.

However, that makes calculating break-even more difficult, since each format sells for a different price. **So, for this exercise we will focus on one format at a time** and find the data we are seeking by format.

Break-Even Point for eBook

Taking the direct eBook costs of $505.75 and adding the indirect costs of $125.39, I readily see that publishing *List of Secrets* in eBook format came to $631.14 of fixed costs.

Let's plug that into the formula:

Break-Even Units = $631.14 / (Price per Unit - Variable Cost per Unit)

Next, I need to consider whether I had any variable costs for this book—were there any costs at all that would have increased **or repeated** for each subsequent unit produced?

Although the product in question is in eBook format, which is sparing me from things like shipping costs, I DO still have to consider royalty split, which is typically 70% for me. And since it recurs with each subsequent unit sold, the part the storefronts keep needs to go in the Variable Cost per Unit spot.

The eBook format of *List of Secrets* sells for $4.99 USD, and at a royalty rate of 70%, that means the storefronts keep $1.50.

So, let's plug in our other known numbers into the equation.

Break-Even Units = $631.14 / ($4.99 - $1.50)
Break-Even Units = $631.14 / $3.49
Break-Even Units = 181 copies

Basically, 181 units of the *List of Secrets* in eBook format need to sell for me to have recouped my costs if I keep my current pricing structure.

Break-Even Point for Paperback

Now let's look at the *paperback* version of the same book where the suggested retail price is $19.99 USD, but it is offered through Ingram Spark at a 53% discount.

For the paperback format, the direct fixed cost total was $405.75, plus the add-in of indirect of $125.39, for a new total of $531.14

Break-Even Units = $531.14 / (Price per Unit - Variable Cost per Unit)

The price per unit has a variant this time, as well - $19.99 less 53%, which brings it down to $9.39.

Break-Even Units = $531.14 / $9.39 - Variable Cost per Unit)

And, I still have variable costs—I have the amount that Ingram Spark will be charging me to print each book that is sold. I know, from what my listed royalty shows, that I am being charged $5.66 for printing for each copy of *List of Secrets*, so, that's my variable cost per unit:

Break-Even Units = $531.14 / $9.39- $5.66
Break-Even Units = $531.14 / $3.73
Break-Even Units = 142 copies

142 copies of my paperback book need to be sold to enable me to recoup my costs if I keep my current pricing structure.

Break-Even Point for Large Print format

Assuming all sales in USD, $24.99 retail price, and 53% discount offered, which results in my getting a $2.52 royalty per sale after $9.22 in print costs. For the large print format, the direct fixed cost total was $605.75, plus the add-in of indirect of $125.39, for a new total of $731.14.

Break-Even Units = $731.14 / $11.74 - $9.22
Break -Even Units = $731.14 / $2.52
Break-Even Units = 290 large-print copies

I need to sell 290 large-print copies to reach break-even point for that format if I keep my current pricing structure.

Pro Tip– If you take the equation and replace this section:
(Price per Unit - Variable Cost per Unit) *with* (Net Profit per Unit) *you will be able to calculate your break-even much faster!*

BREAKING EVEN OR BREAKING YOUR MIND?

MLL

If you had difficulty with this chapter, I advise going back and re-reading it again slowly. I know it's something I had to do. But I'm glad I did it. Because it really helped.

You see, understanding your break-even point for a book is a critical and fundamental aspect of managing and understanding your author business.

D.F. broke down her break-even points by format. That's not something I'd ever done before, except, perhaps for audiobooks, because they were usually added well after I'd already earned-out the costs of publishing a novel.

But from this chapter, I took the learnings of cost allocating discussed in Chapter Four and then used D.F.'s more complex use of allocating those costs across all formats.

What it helped me see, in this case, when allocating editorial and cover design costs across all formats, that my eBook costs are actually lower than originally estimated, but the costs for my audiobook are higher than previously noted.

Is there something from this chapter you can apply to your own specific calculation models?

One extra note. Please don't panic, or beat yourself up, or worry about going back and re-doing all your previous work and calculations.

If this is new knowledge, maybe, like me, be able to apply these calculations on your **next** project.

That's still a huge win and insight for you to take forward in your author business.

CHAPTER SIX:

Profits & Other Metrics, Part 2

DFH

Calculating Gross and Net Income

First, here's what each term means:

Gross Income is what you see after you subtract your business's *Cost of Sales* from your *Sales Revenue*.

Net Income goes a step further. Net Income is *Sales Revenue* minus *Cost of Sales* minus *Operating Expenses*. OR, *Gross Income* minus *Operating Expenses*.

 Gross Income is straightforward—you tally up your sales revenue and you subtract your direct costs to make the product.
 Now, to find each in a real-life scenario!
 For example: I have had $2,535.39 in eBook sales for *List of Secrets,* and we know from looking at break-even point earlier that my direct costs to publish *List* as an eBook came to $505.75.

So, $2,535.39 minus $505.75 = **Gross income (or profit) of $2,029.64 for eBook sales of this title.**

To find the Net income (or profit/loss) on *List of Secrets* eBook sales, I would *also* need to subtract out the allocated indirect costs of $125.39 PLUS any other expense items not already accounted for—namely, marketing.

In the case of this eBook title, I landed a BookBub Featured Deal specific to this book that cost me $650, so, I need to account for that expense, as well.

$2,535.39 minus $505.75 minus $125.39 minus $650 = **$1,254.25 Net income (profit)** on eBook sales of that title.

***

Calculating Margin

Margin is essentially the difference between revenue and expenses and is usually displayed as a percentage rather than in currency format.

To find **Gross margin**, gross profit is divided by revenue, then multiplied by 100 to get a percentage.

So, in the *List of Secrets* eBook example from before, the gross margin would be:

$$(\text{Gross profit} / \text{Revenue}) \times 100$$
$$(\$2,029.64 / \$2,535.39) \times 100$$
$$0.80052 \times 100 = \textbf{80.05\% gross margin}$$

To find **Net margin**, divide Net profit by revenue and multiply by 100, like so:

(Net profit / Revenue) X 100
($1,254.25 / $2,535.39) X 100
0.49469 x 100 = **49.47% net margin**

***

Net Return, Return on Investment, and Payback Period

Other useful calculations for authors to know are **Net Return, Return on Investment (or ROI), and Payback Period.** These three concepts are interrelated.

Net return

Net return is what you made (or lost) on an activity after you subtract out the costs of that activity from the results of that activity.

A real-life author world example of this is landing a BookBub Featured Deal.

If the deal costs you $1,000 and your sales from that Featured Deal totaled $1,400 then your **net return** on that activity is $400.

The result minus the cost = your net return, whether it's good (a positive number), or bad (a negative number.)

Return on Investment (ROI)

Return on Investment (ROI) is shown as a percentage, and in basic terms, it's a measurement of how well a certain activity did.

To find your ROI percentage for your BookBub Featured Deal, you would divide the $400 by your initial costs of $1000: $400 / $1000 = 0.4

Then multiply by 100 to get to a percentage: 0.4 x 100 = 40%.

Just like net return, **ROI can also be negative,** which is how you know that whatever activity you did wasn't a good thing for your business.

Take the following example:

You use XYZ company's paid newsletter. It costs you $100, and you get $50 in sales from that promotion.

Using the formulas, here's how that net return and ROI turns out:

(Result — Cost) = net return
$50 - $100 = ($50)* net return

net return / initial cost = ROI
($50)* / $100 = (0.5) x 100 = (50%)* ROI

*Please note that the brackets around the numeric value in the formula above are commonly used in accounting to denote negative values. Thus ($50) above means -$50, or negative fifty dollars and (50%) means -50%, or negative fifty percent.

Payback Period

Payback Period simply refers to the length of time that it takes for an investment or activity to reach break-even point, or in other words, how long it takes to recover that cost. **Typically, this is measured in years**.

In the author world, the best example I can think of where **P**ayback Period will probably stretch out longer than a year would be audiobooks.

So, let's use my first audiobook production as our example.

I spent $2,000 to get my first audiobook made, and in the first year of its publication, I made $150 in royalties from that audiobook. (Sadly, this truly *is* a real-life example of something from my own author career. But if it helps people learn, I'm all for sharing my data.)

So, to find **Payback Period**, I need to do this:

Initial investment / royalty per year = Payback Period
$2,000 / $150 = 13.33 years!

Unless I manage to sell more copies and get that yearly royalty number to increase, my audiobook investment's payback period is more than thirteen years. Sigh.

***

A WORD ON GOALS

MLL

That last example from D.F. could be a dramatic culture shock to you, dear reader, particularly if you aren't clear on both your short-term and your long-term goals.

Whatever your own personal goals are is for you—and you alone—to decide. Even if those goals aren't to make a full-time living (or even a part-time living) off the sales of your books, it is really important to understand what those goals are as well as the costs, expenditures, and payback values for your writing.

If, for example, your goal is to write books to make the world a better place, publishing them as permanently free eBooks, regardless of what it costs, there are still costs involved, and the business of conducting that operation.

Just keep your goals in mind.

And not just the big and long-term ones. But the smaller ones along the way.

When I do a 1:1 consultation with an author, one of the first questions I usually ask for our hour-long chat is what they hope to leave that meeting with. IE, what is the ultimate goal for that short period of time and the money they have invested.

All of it requires some sort of budget. Budgets of time, money, and other resources. And that's what's covered next.

CHAPTER SEVEN:
Budget: It's Not a Dirty Word

DFH

Budget. Just the word itself fills many with dread.

And, admittedly, a lot of times it is not much fun, because we always seem to have a finite amount of income and an ever-increasing list of things we need or want to spend that precious limited resource of ours on.

But developing a budget for your author business is crucial. Without building one (and then sticking to it), spending can escalate out of control and obliterate any forward progress you might have made toward reaching that all-important goal, which is to turn your passion for writing into a self-sustaining and profitable business.

I would even suggest to you that keeping two finite resources in mind while you build your budget is optimal—your money, and your *time*. Because everything costs something—time or money. The two are not mutually exclusive. They're quite interconnected, and I will explain that more in a moment.

Another huge point to remember is—a budget is *not* a static document. This is not a 'one-and-done forever and ever' thing; it is intended to be a living, breathing document that can be reviewed and adjusted as your situation grows or changes.

After all, with each book you publish, your costs (and hopefully, your budget dollars) will, overall, generally increase, right? So—why would you apply a two-book budget scenario to a twenty-book situation?

So, D.F., what's the magic formula for authors? Lay it on me.

Well, there *are* some existing strategies out in the world—the "50/30/20 method," popularized by Senator Elizabeth Warren's 2005 book *All Your Worth: The Ultimate Lifetime Money Plan*, is one of them. Others advocate the "80/20" method, which is a model based upon early 20th century Italian economist Vilfredo Parteo's concepts.

But these are geared toward *personal* budgeting, and as an author (and business owner) you need to get into a *business* mindset.

And generally, in the business world most budgets are structured one of four ways: incremental, activity-based, value proposition, or zero-based.

Incremental budgeting takes the prior financial period's data and uses it as the basis for the next period's budget number. While this approach is useless at start-up, it is a good one once you've got an initial data set built up to work with. Most of the companies I've worked for as an Accounting Manager use this approach—an "x + z%" view.

Activity-based budgeting begins from the *opposite* direction of incremental. Rather than looking at historical data to build a budgeting model, this approach sets the desired end goal, and then works backward from that to figure out what's needed to reach that goal—and the costs incurred to do so.

Value proposition budgeting (personally, my least favorite) is about questioning things included in the budget calculation to make sure that everything listed drives value for the business.

Lastly, *zero-based budgeting* is a quite common approach and assumes that everything starts from nothing and must be built up.

Personally, the zero-based budgeting approach resonated with me the best when I first began my author journey, because I was starting out brand new, so, 'assuming' everything needed to be built wasn't necessary—I *was* at zero.

BUT—I won't lie and tell you that there's a specific setup that you *must* follow to get this done. In good conscience, I can't, because each author's situation is different.

One person may be financially able to easily set aside 30% of their budget per month for marketing. For another person, even trying to set aside 5% a month for marketing might bring relentless anxiety. (Been there, done that, and yes, it was *super* stressful.)

One person reading this right now may have a background in graphic design that enables them to build their own quality covers, and so that individual would have no need to set aside funds for cover design. Whereas someone like me, who struggles with spatial orientation and who cannot draw her way out of a paper bag, might be better served hiring someone else to build the cover.

An author that's been doing this a while may have their business to where it is already 'self-sustaining' from an income and expense standpoint. Others reading this book may be just getting started on their path.

So, what budgeting boils down to is this: Your resources are your own; they are unique to you. And therefore—using an old analogy and thinking of it like a pie—you must slice up that pie in a way that is the most feasible for *you*.

Chasing someone else's recommendation of how to best allocate *your* resources is, in my view, not the way to proceed. After all, they do not know the nuances particular to *your* situation, nor does 'one size fits all' advice take into consideration what your personal *risk tolerance level* is.

Regardless of how you slice up that pie, your budget should have the following characteristics:

1) *It should be realistic.* One of the fastest ways to help ensure that you do not follow a budget is to build one that's unreasonable.

2) *It should be flexible.* You need the ability to tweak it as your business grows and changes. Personally, I tend to favor using percentages rather than currency amounts, so that my budget scales up or down more easily.

3) *It should be easily understood.* There's no need to doll it all up. Keep your approach straightforward.

4) *It should be mindful.* Being an author is one of a handful of professions where the money we make involves two catches:

   a. The money we make is not paid to us weekly or bi-weekly, as it would be at a 'day job'. We get our money anywhere from thirty to ninety days after we've earned it. Your budget needs to take this into account.

   b. Royalty payments typically have zero taxes withheld, no matter what country you live in - or where the sales occurred. Your budget should include a slice specifically allotted to address that, so that you are not caught short later. (*As with all things tax-related, please consult a **pro in your area** to make sure you're on track on this point!*)

***

A General Approach for Start-Up

I opted to begin with the *zero-based budgeting* approach when I first started this journey. And I am going to presume as I walk you through how to do this that you are exactly where I was — no separate income stream available with which to launch your business.

If your situation was like mine, you have to figure out how much of your *household's* resources can be diverted over to fund your author career.

So, the first step is to total up all income sources (use *take-home* pay, not gross pay, and do NOT include things that cannot be routinely counted on, such as bonuses or overtime pay).

Next, subtract out all your 'real-life' expenses — mortgage/rent, vehicle payments, utilities, groceries, all of it. Don't forget items like dues and subscriptions, your cell phone, and things that don't happen monthly, such as car maintenance items. Take those randomly occurring things and divide that cost by twelve to get a 'per month' number, and add them in.

What is left over is commonly referred to as 'disposable income'. That amount (or a portion of it) is the amount that you can *comfortably* stand to shift out of your 'household' bucket and put toward your business.

My scenario:

The first thing I did was sit down and look at my income from all sources — my husband and I were both working full-time day jobs. I did the legwork and calculated all our 'real-life' monthly expenses — mortgage payment, utilities, car payments, insurance, groceries, and so on.

Once I had that number, I subtracted it from our bring-home pay, and I was left with our 'disposable income'.

Then I asked myself: *How much of this disposable income can I <u>comfortably divert</u> over into my author stuff without disrupting the real-life finances?*

This was an important question for me to answer because this was, in part, my naturally conservative risk tolerance level manifesting itself.

In my case, I was only comfortable with allocating a maximum of $325 a month at that point in time.

Not to mention that at that point, I had a 'quasi' budget, but not really any clear direction. My little boat was adrift. So, the next step was to *set a goal* — some landmark to point my sailboat toward, as it were.

What did I want to achieve?

The initial answer was, get my first book out onto the market in eBook form, and go from there.

But that was only *part* of the answer, because without knowing *what it costs* to publish a single eBook, *there's no way to form a battle plan to accomplish it.*

So, the next thing I did was take a hard look at the costs involved in reaching that initial goal - publishing a single eBook — and I did so with the <u>initial presumption that I would NOT be doing *any* of it myself,</u> so that I could arrive at an 'absolute worst-case scenario' number to work with.

I did some shopping and came up with average costs for each facet of what is *typically* involved in producing one eBook in my primary genre, which is thriller/suspense. Those were:

Cover design—I found the prices to be anywhere from $75 - $1,000. And I will be honest, I just about had a stroke when I saw how expensive they can get! I opted to go with $200 estimated costs for a single book e-cover in my budgeting and planning.

Editing / Proofing—Most of the editors and proofreaders that I researched charged a flat rate per word or per page (it is commonly agreed that 250 words equals one page) or a flat rate per hour.

Since I had not quite figured out the length of the final version of my book, I ball parked it at 75,000 words.

But, I also learned that there were distinct types of editing—and each typically had a different rate—so that made life even more interesting!

Finally, I said 'enough', and I plugged in the average rate per word: 75000*.025 = $1,875.

Blurb writing—the median rate I found was $175.

Formatting—I found that people on average will spend up to $500 on formatting. Some will spend more, but it depends a lot, I think, on the genre (i.e., fiction versus nonfiction) and whether pictures, charts, and graphs are a part of the manuscript.

When I sat down and added up what I had found, this was the initial result:

Cover	$200
Editing	$1,875
Blurb	$175
Formatting	$500
Total	**$2,750**

And I will be honest—when I first saw that number, I almost did not proceed with becoming self-published. Because that is a *chunk* of money—in my world, that's more than our house and our vehicle payments combined for one month! Add on top of that my natural inclination toward being risk-averse, and I was seriously having second thoughts.

So, I immediately took a step back and thought to myself, 'What on this list can I reasonably accomplish on my own until such time as my budget can be bigger?'

Or in other words: what can I spend my *time* on rather than my *money*, at least at first, to help me accomplish my goals? What strengths do I possess that I can leverage here?

For me personally, the answer at the start of my career was 'handle the editing, formatting, and writing the blurb myself.' Before diverting over into accounting, I was an English major in college and have always had extraordinarily strong writing skills, especially regarding proper spelling, punctuation, and the like.

My initial plan of self-edit also involved using Microsoft Word's free built-in 'read aloud' feature, which helped me catch and fix awkward phrasing, transposed words, and other things. After that, I asked someone else whom I trust to proofread my manuscript as well.

The one thing that I already knew about myself is it would never be possible for me to generate my own cover—as I mentioned previously, I simply do not have the skill set needed—so that piece I would *have* to delegate to a paid third party.

Was deciding to do some things myself the best course of action *for my work*? Maybe and maybe not. But at the time, to make a go of this, I opted to make that choice—in other words, I set my *risk tolerance level* accordingly.

Now, I knew that what I understood about self-publishing could fit into a thimble with plenty of room left over, so, rather than putting room in my budget for, say, a blurb, I opted to instead invest in some learning materials. I did that primarily by joining several Facebook author groups at no cost, but, I also joined ALLi.

Armed with all that, in the very first month of my author business, my budget in early 2019 was allocated like this:

Total budget per month to work with:	$325
Cover design	($200)
Subtotal left	$125
ALLi Membership	($119)
Subtotal left - Month One	$6

You read that right, friends and neighbors. According to my budget, I would have had six dollars left that first month to work with—barely enough for a meal. But I got lucky, and my first cover only cost me around $125. So, I was able to add back $75 into my budget, which put me at $81 left to work with for the first month.

But I knew going forward that I would not always be able to continue to do certain things myself; at some point, it would not only benefit my *craft* much more if I financially invested in some of the other facets, but that eventually I would also not be able to spare the *time* to do those things myself.

It's important to point out that at this stage, with only one book in the works, there was not much point (in my mind, anyway) in even budgeting anything for marketing, since there were not yet any subsequent books for people to read through to! So, I focused instead on building the best possible infrastructure that I could and getting the next eBook's cover paid for—and the moment I began to see sales, I *also* earmarked and set aside money for the inevitable—tax season.

I tell you all that to tell you this—regardless of your approach and how you choose to slice up your pie, my *strong recommendation is that you, <u>within thirty days of that first sale</u>, begin to set aside anywhere from 22% to 30% of the revenue you make.* It is much easier to do this as things go along rather than waiting until it's time to pay the tax man. An excellent method of doing this is to set up a recurring auto-transfer from one account to another—and then spot check the balance, say, every quarter, against the revenue you have received, and adjust the amount transferred accordingly.

And as I've said elsewhere in this book (and will probably repeat at least once more later), **it is best to consult a tax pro in your area to make sure you're on the right path for your needs and situation.**

A General Approach *after* Start-Up

For those readers who are past the start-up point, remember: Your budget is a living, breathing thing, not a one-off static event. And *"forecasting" is simply your best estimated guess of where you'd like to land at some future point.*

For scaling and forecasting, I personally find that it is most helpful to implement a combination of the *incremental* and *activity-based* budgeting approaches.

First, look back—ideally, twelve months of data, but even six months' worth is a good start.

And here's the activity that needs to happen at this point. Run some calculations. Did you stay within, or blow out, those percentages you gave yourself for cover design, or for formatting, or for marketing?

(Hint: Generally speaking, it can be the marketing slice of pie that tends to be the most badly behaved if not monitored closely.)

If something in your budgeted plans went wonky, analyze your data (which we will walk through more of how to do as we continue in this book) and see if you can pinpoint where it went off course—and the results. Did you exceed your allotted spend amount(s), and if so, *why*?

Was it a 'not great' thing, like a cost-per-click ad that got out of control, or was it because you landed that coveted BookBub Featured Deal?

Did a planned cover or editing cost you more than you expected, or were you blindsided by an awesome idea for a brand-new story (or series) that had you so fired up to get it started that you went ahead and bought a cover for it, too?

Remember, *good things can also alter our trajectory*, just like negative things can.

Once you've researched the past, take up the *activity-based* budgeting mindset and look forward. What is the next goal you'd like to reach? Plot it out, work out what the costs are to get there, and then, compare *those* figures against your historical data to calculate the distance between the two. *That's* your next budget concept: Slice up your pie in the way that's most likely to get you to that goal.

A Reminder for All

Keep in mind that sometimes it's unexpected things that only come to light *after* our work is out in the marketplace that cause us to have to rethink, and possibly adjust, what we're doing.

For example—in my case, I realized in the fall of 2020 that the first set of covers I had out in the world on my (by that time) four thriller books, while pretty, just weren't hitting the right marks.

So, I had to take a deep breath and regroup—and make some hard choices, because although my available budget had grown some, I was still having to be careful.

Part of doing that was making the conscious decision to suspend any further attempts at ad spend on that series *or* on getting my other pen name's inaugural series off the ground.

Instead, I chose to redirect all my spending for the next two months over into getting my thriller covers dialed in—and I would not have been able to do that if my budget was rigid. But because I understood that at its core *a budget is a guideline, not a carved-in-stone commitment*, I could make the transition.

And making that adjustment—taking the time to look at my data and realizing "I have to make this change" and then following through—is what broke my sales wide open. Redirecting those budget dollars to new covers for my four existing thriller books wound up landing me a BookBub Featured Deal on book one of that series—and the sales from that put me in the black to end 2020, something that had not happened often at all to that point.

Those sales enabled me to channel *more* budget dollars into getting my other pen name's series off the ground. They also enabled me to *finally* turn some of the editing items over to someone else—which meant that my stories became even higher-quality reads for my fans.

Budget Rule Breakdown

MLL

Many budgeting rules have been tossed around, debated, and discussed over the years and are commonly known by those who are in the business of accounting or who have studied it. But I was unfamiliar with them so I thought I would quickly outline the ones D.F. mentions early in this chapter in case that is also useful to you.

The 50/30/20 budgeting rule divides your after-tax income into three categories: 50% for needs, 30% for wants, and 20% for savings. "Needs" would include obligatory expenses such as mortgage and rent.

The 80/20 budgeting rule means you put 20% of your after-tax income into savings. The remaining 80% is for spending.

This is a simplified overview, of course. Some detailed financial plans might re-allocate that 20% "savings" portion to include "savings and debt-repayment." This is because debt negates savings, so eliminating it ensures the integrity of that savings value.

The key, in most of these plans or rules, is investing a specific portion for the future. Not unlike the way D.F. suggests investing in your author business.

CHAPTER EIGHT:
Marketing: NOT a how-to guide.
A how & why to monitor your results guide

DFH

Ah, marketing. My least favorite part of authorship. But, it's necessary for all of us, at least to some extent.

The good thing about marketing as an author is that there is more than one way to get the word out about your books.

And, the bad thing about marketing as an author is that there is more than one way to get the word out about your books.

Some people swear by the 'cost-per-click ad'.

Others vehemently lean as far away from cost-per-click ads as possible and instead use what are called "paid newsletters" such as Fussy Librarian.

Still others prefer Facebook, Instagram, Twitter, Tik-Tok, Pinterest, and other social media outlets to connect to potential new superfans.

Building and maintaining an author website and a newsletter or blog that draws subscribers is yet another popular marketing method.

There's also the raging debate about whether one should use the 'loss leader' concept by offering a free book to tempt possible new superfans into giving your work a try.

And of course, lots of authors use a combined strategy, layering more than one of these approaches.

I like to view the entire concept of marketing in this industry as a buffet—you need to try different tactics for yourself and *see what works best for you*. (But, stay true to your goals, your budget, and your risk tolerance level.)

But, D.F., I hear people swear by (insert marketing technique here).

My advice? Familiarize yourself with the concept behind each available marketing tool, and weigh the pros and cons (and costs, both in time and in money) of each as they relate to your stated goals and objectives. Then, try some out, and see what each technique accomplishes with *your* books and targeting *your* ideal readers.

At the end of it all, you need to do what resonates with you. If you find that you hate a particular method, don't force yourself to do it, plain and simple.

Now, let's look at some pros and cons of different marketing avenues, including cost (this *is* an accounting book, so, we need to tick that 'everything costs something' box, right? Right.)

Cost-per-Click Ads (CPC)

A checkmark in the 'pro' column for cost-per-click ads is that they can reach a *huge* audience. They can also be fine-tuned so that you can really dial into specific categories and ensure that you are targeting the groups most likely to pick up and read your book.

However, cost-per-click finesse can be hard to master. Often, it requires loads of testing and tweaking—and that costs both money and time, not only to 'dial in' your ad in the first place, but to monitor it on a regular basis and adjust it as needed if you see that results have slowed or stopped.

Cost-per-click ad costs are **variable**, and if not tracked can get out of control quickly, so, if you opt to include this in your arsenal, be prepared to watch your ads' performance closely.

Paid Newsletters

Paid newsletters have one big advantage over cost-per-click ads, and that is that paid newsletters are a **fixed** price per booking. This makes budgeting your ad spend (and staying within said budget) much easier.

The trade off, quite frankly, is reach. Paid newsletters simply do not have the reach potential that cost-per-click ads do. The biggest 'paid newsletter' of them all is the BookBub Featured Deal, and at the time of writing this chapter, BookBub's largest genre-specific subscriber list topped three million people. While impressive, that's still a drop in the bucket compared to the *billions* of folks currently on the planet.

The other drawback to the paid newsletter approach is timing; many of them limit how often a title can run in a calendar year, while a cost-per-click ad can run twenty-four hours a day, 365 days a year.

Social Media Outlets

Free in terms of financial cost but can be outrageously hard on your *time* budget. You're also at the mercy of the service provider—for example, I believe we all probably know at least one person whose account has been suspended, even temporarily, on Facebook.

Your Own Website / Blog / Newsletter

Can be a bit cost-intensive to start-up, but if done correctly (i.e., *buy* your domain name so that it's 'locked in' for you) it works quite well. Website maintenance costs are typically incurred annually, and newsletter service providers (such as MailerLite and Mailchimp) are typically billed to you monthly.

Regarding your website—it can be a bit more time-intensive to maintain/update the site, build blog posts, and so on, but the trade-off is that this is marketing 'real estate' that *you* own and control.

***

Calculating Costs of Marketing

This next bit will focus specifically on cost-per-click ads and paid newsletters—the two marketing types that *typically we connect to a specific title* at any given point in time.

There are four things you want to try to measure with BOTH types of ads, if possible:

1) Cost-per-click
2) Cost-per-download / sale
3) Net return
4) ROI

For Cost-Per-Click Ads:

Cost-per-click is simply the amount you've invested divided by the number of clicks your ad generates. If I spend $75 on a cost-per-click ad that results in 125 people clicking the 'call-to-action' button on that ad, then my cost-per-click is:

$75 / 125 = 0.60 per *click.*

That number in and of itself might make some people decide to stop running that ad. But I really do need to look past that and figure net return and ROI if possible before I decide to pull that plug.

Having said that—if that ad is on a free book, then cost-per-sale calculation is pretty much moot unless I can track any extraneous sales of my *other* books back to that same ad. This can be difficult to do.

But let's assume for teaching purposes that the book my CPC ad is running on is NOT free, it's $4.99.

If 35 of those people who clicked the 'call to action' button on my cost-per-click ad buy *that* book, then it cost me:

$75 / 35 = $2.14 per *sale* to run that ad.

If the average royalty on a $4.99 eBook sale for me is $3.49 per book sold, then those 35 people made me $122.15.

So, now I can calculate net return and ROI:

Net return is $122.15 - $75 = $47.15

And your ROI would be $47.15 / $75 = 0.628 x 100 = 62.8%.

So, while 0.60 per click or $2.14 per sale might seem daunting, the point of all this is that you really need to look at the resulting data *from more than one direction* to get a good grasp on whether or not to continue that ad spend.

For a $4.99 book, those numbers become more palatable because your royalty per book is still higher than either 'per click' or 'per sale' spend.

However, if you're advertising a book at a lower price, (and therefore at a lower royalty), then you might be better served to at least tweak if not stop that ad, because at some point your cost per sale *will* overtake your net profit.

For Paid Newsletter Ads:

(NOTE: There is only one paid newsletter company that I can think of that shows you the *number of clicks* your listing got with them—Book Raider.)

As for sales or downloads, you will need to pull data from each retailer where your books are sold and assimilate more information yourself (unless you use a service such as ScribeCount, which I will talk more about later.)

For our purposes, we are going to assume that the paid newsletter was NOT for a free book, but for a $2.99 book.

So, let's say that I booked a promo on Book Raider, and I included links to five different storefronts for my book.

The promo costs me $60, and I received 842 total clicks across all storefronts. My 'cost-per-click' for the Book Raider ad overall is:

$60 / 842 = 0.07 per *click*.

And for fun, let's say that a couple of days later my sales data updates, and I discover that of those 842 total clicks, I sold a total of 69 books across all storefronts.

If my royalty rate on a $2.99 book is $2.09, then those 69 sales netted me $144.42. Not too shabby on a $60 investment!

So now, let's calculate the net return and ROI, shall we?

$144.42 - $60 = $84.42 net return

ROI = $84.42 / $60 = 141%

This kind of result for me personally would land this paid newsletter in my 'awesome tools' category, and I would utilize it again.

***

Calculating Readthrough

"Readthrough" is the measurement of how many of the people who buy or download the first book in a series go on to read the rest of that series. And typically, it's quite a difference when it involves a free first-in-series than a paid one.

I have a couple of notes for you here before we get started:

- Regardless of book one's free or paid status, it is most helpful to perform this analysis with a *large* data set: i.e., all titles involved for which you seek to calculate readthrough have been published and available on the market for *at least* six months. Doing so helps level out any spikes, such as paid promos or specials run, and it also helps account for staggered release dates. Let's face it, you will never have as many sales of book six as you will book one, given that most likely book one was out long before book six was published.

- This calculation's results are not set in stone; other factors may come into play, so, read-through is meant to be an estimate.

When your first book is PAID:

We will look at a PAID first in series to start.

Let's say that we pulled data and found out that in a six-month period, for a six-book series, sales looked like this:

Book One = 520 sales
Book Two = 334 sales
Book Three = 261 sales
Book Four = 216 sales
Book Five = 187 sales
Book Six = 117 sales

The method by which to calculate read-through from one book to the next is as follows:

# of units of book B / # of units of book A

So, if you had 520 sales of book one, and 334 sales of book two, then your read-through from book one to book two would be:

334 / 520 = 64.2%

To find out an estimate of how many of those people read **book three**, divide *book three by book two*, like so:

261 sales of book three / 334 sales of book two = 78.1%
From book to book, read-through would look like this:

Book 1 to Book 2 = 334 / 520 = 64.2%
Book 2 to Book 3 =261 / 334 = 78.1%
Book 3 to Book 4 = 216 / 261 = 82.8%
Book 4 to Book 5 = 187 / 216 = 86.6%
Book 5 to Book 6 = 117 / 187 = 62.6%

And if you wanted to find out an estimate of how many of your readers who picked up book one *read all the way through your series*, you would divide each subsequent book's numbers by *book one's* number:

Book One = 520 divided by 520 = 100%
Book Two = 334 divided by 520 = 64.2%
Book Three = 261 divided by 520 = 50.2%
Book Four = 216 divided by 520 = 41.5%
Book Five = 187 divided by 520 = 36.0%
Book Six = 117 divided by 520 = 22.5%

So, *in theory*, 22.5% of the people who buy book one will read the rest of the series.

When your first book is FREE:
What about when your first in series is free? That *will* skew your numbers, but don't panic—in a 'free first in series' scenario, it's quite common for read-through from book one to book two to drop down as low as 1-2 percent.
Why, you ask?

Volume, plain and simple. For example, if you land a Bookbub Featured Deal on your first in series and it's free, that will usually result in thousands of downloads. Even using a combination of paid newsletters, such as Fussy Librarian, can result in big numbers.

So, let's take those same book data numbers we used a minute ago, but let's add in 10,000 downloads of a free book one to the mix:

Book One = 10,520 divided by 10,520 = 100%
Book Two = 334 divided by 10,520 = 3.2%
Book Three = 261 divided by 10,520 = 2.5%
Book Four = 216 divided by 10,520 = 2.1%
Book Five = 187 divided by 10,520 = 1.8%
Book Six = 117 divided by 10,520 = 1.1%

In this scenario, only an estimated 1.1% of those 10,520 people will read your entire series.

Wow, D.F. those percentages are horrible! Why would anyone do a free first in series if read-through is going to be so low?

Here's why: in the second scenario, <u>ten thousand more people</u> picked up your book.

So, by having your first in series free, you've just gotten the attention of an additional 10,000 people that could read all the way through your series, and if the rest of your titles are full-priced, that is a healthy number of sales.

And now, let's look at the typically most prolific 'paid newsletter' of all—BookBub Featured Deals (BBFD).

For my main genre (thriller) a BBFD can garner an average of 31,900 downloads of a free book, per BookBub's own pricing and statistics page. For our purposes, let's use that average.

So, factoring those in:

Book One = 31,900 + 520 sales = 32,420
Book Two = 334 sales
Book Three = 261 sales
Book Four = 216 sales
Book Five = 187 sales
Book Six = 117 sales

Which makes read-through look like this from book one to book two:

334 / 32,420= 1.03%

And like this from book one through the rest of the series:

Book One = 32,420 divided by 32,420 = 100%
Book Two = 334 divided by 32,420 = 1.03%
Book Three = 261 divided by 32,420 = 0.81%
Book Four = 216 divided by 32,420 = 0.67%
Book Five = 187 divided by 32,420 = 058%
Book Six = 117 divided by 32,420 = 0.36%
0.36% of 32,420, or 117 people, are *statistically* likely to read all the way through your series.

My point in showing you all this simply:

When 32,420 people pick up book one, it doesn't take nearly as high a percentage to achieve the same results as it does when there's only 520 people.

NOTE: *Keep in mind that calculating read-through is simply statistical analysis, nothing more, and it is certainly not a guarantee of future sales behavior. There is nothing in all this that means you will ever only get x% of your readers continuing in your series. <u>Readthrough is meant as a baseline only</u> and can be affected by marketing and promos of subsequent books in series, among other things.*

***

Special note about marketing to gain new subscribers

Occasionally, you may want to invest in marketing that increases the number of followers you have on a platform (such as BookBub) or that subscribe to your newsletter, rather than promoting a specific title in your catalogue.

The cost to measure in this instance is *per person*. For example, if I spend $25 to be involved in a newsletter builder campaign, and 267 new subscribers join my mailing list, then each new addition to my subscriber list costs me $0.09. And if you have a subscription to Bookfunnel or Story Origin that allows you to participate in as many promos as you want for a fixed monthly rate, then you would simply divide the monthly rate by the number of new subscribers that month to find 'cost-per-subscriber.'

***

Now I want to provide four gentle reminders specific to marketing. The first two relate to *all* marketing types, and the two relate to marketing a free or 'permafree' book and doing a storefront's in-house promotion, respectively.

1). As an accountant, I will always, *always* caution you against funding any type of marketing with a credit card. The reason for this is simple—unlike your bank debit card or PayPal account, credit cards involve interest that compounds *daily*.

What this means is that each day, the interest charged adds to your principal balance owed. The only way to mitigate this is to pay the balance off in full every month. And if you're able to do that, great. But if not, that compounded interest can compound the hits to your budget over time, so be mindful of what you use those card(s) for.

2). Take anyone who you hear say 'I made $10,000 this month' with a grain of salt unless they go on to divulge the entire story. BOTH sides, sales AND expenses. You will encounter these folks, if you haven't already, in some author groups. And while the sales figures they're divulging might sound impressive, you need to keep in mind one simple question—is that *gross*, or *net*? *Before* expenses, or *after*? Because **everything costs something,** and in my personal point of view, someone spending $9,500 to make $10,000 in sales is just not that impressive.

3). Do not be disappointed if you do not 'earn out', or in other words, recoup what you spend, in a single day on marketing a book (particularly a free or permafree one), for two main reasons:

a) Some of the people who get that Fussy Librarian or Book Raider or BookBub Featured Deal email with your title included may not even *open* that email for a few days.

b) Marketing a free book is a little different than advertising a paid book. When you market a free book, *sell-through and read-through to other books in your catalogue is what will help determine whether that promotion was successful or not, and quite frankly, that can take some time.* Not every reader who snatches up your free offering will read it right away, and not every reader will immediately go buy your other books.

You need to go into these types of marketing moves armed with the expectation that quite often it takes a bit of time to recoup that initial investment you have made.

4). My last piece of advice is this: *just because a promotion is "free to join" money-wise does not mean it is at no cost to you.*

Remember, **everything costs something**.

So, if you are a wide author who lists your books with Kobo, as an example, you can join one of their in-house promotions, and a lot of them are zero cost out-of-pocket. *But the tradeoff is a reduction in royalty rate* paid to you each time your book sells.

REMINDER: Everything Costs Something

MLL

I just wanted to reiterate the last message from D.F. in this chapter (**Everything costs something**) and how that relates to decisions that I make in my author business.

Though I have experimented with, and continue to experiment with various Amazon Advertising, Facebook, and BookBub Ads, one thing that's needed to ensure those ads are successful is regular and ongoing analysis, measurement, and tweaking.

In most cases, you can't just set it up and forget it.

So, while measuring the end results of something like read-thru in order to determine the effectiveness of the ad when it comes down to monetary costs and the growth of your readership and sales (as D.F. outlines above) is important, there's an additional element that I realize always ends up costing me far more.

My time.

Because I'm not good at numbers, and because my time is pretty sparse—let's be honest here: nobody has more time than they need to balance all the work/life/family responsibilities on their plates—I regularly struggle with the time it takes to do the analysis of many of the CPC and CPM type ads.

If I budget $100, for example, to run an Amazon Ad, then take the time to determine what I believe—likely through the use of tools like Publisher Rocket—the best keywords should be, there's still additional time that needs to be invested in reviewing the results of the ad and then adjusting and tweaking.

That daily adjusting and analysis ends up usually taking an additional hour out of every day. And, after a week, that's a full 7 hours that I could have been spending writing.

I've long loved the term WIBBOW (attributed to Scott William Carter) that I heard about years ago at a Master Class taught by Kristine Kathryn Rusch and Dean Wesley Smith.

WIBBOW = Would I Be Better Off Writing?

Because we all know that one of the best ways to earn more income as a writer is having more products out there. That's the whole reason why calculating your series sell-thru is so important.

But if I'm taking that much time to do in depth analytics and constantly tweaking and adjusting ads that require it, I'm taking away from time spent writing.

If I can write 1000 words an hour on average, then 7 hours spent adjusting ads could be (and thank goodness this is easy math, even for someone like me) 7000 words. That might be a short story, or a chapter or perhaps two chapters in a book.

And, since I don't pay anyone else to write the words for me—I can pay an editor, I can pay a cover designer, I can pay an admin assistant to do some maintenance tasks, but I write my own books, so I have to have the time to do that myself—that's 7 lost hours.

So, often, when deciding what types of ads and mar-keting I'm willing to invest in, that $100 budgeted for an ad might (in my case) be better invested towards a news-letter like BookBub, BargainBooksy, Fussy Librarian, or Book Raid.

Because with those newsletters, I pay my $100 (or whatever I've budgeted), then *they* do all the heavy lift-ing. Because of the value I place on the time I spent gen-erating new material, or new IP (Intellectual Property) that I can earn money from.

It's something worth considering.

And it's so important, we dedicate the next chapter to that topic.

CHAPTER NINE:
Know Your Worth—and not just from a dollar and cents standpoint!

DFH

Knowing your worth is so much more than just sales revenue; it encompasses some massively important things that we cannot see or touch; namely, our intellectual property, and our time.

And both of those things—Intellectual Property, or IP, and time—can be extremely difficult to assign a concrete value, because the value of each is very subjective.

Regarding IP valuation, there are two principal methods by which people attempt to assign concrete values—the **income method**, and the **market method**.

The **income method** calculates potential future cashflow derived from the work (typically, within a 10-year period), and the **market method** looks at historical data of similar IP having been bought and sold in a business transaction to figure out the value.

So, using the **income method**, if I have a six-book series that's made me $2,000 in royalties a year for the last two years, one could *reasonably assume* that the value of that IP could possibly be $20,000 ($2,000 per year for 10 years).

The **market method** would be extremely interesting to try to use in the author realm, because it's only the 'mega pay-days' that seem to make the public airwaves, and even then, only sometimes. Unlike publicly traded businesses, when an 'acquisition' or transfer of IP takes place in the writing world, the details of the 'sale' aren't readily available for dissection.

My advice? **When in doubt, talk with somebody fluent in IP valuations.**

Now, on to time.

For most professions, there's at least one standardized salary guide that one can look at to get a feel for a median range in a certain geographic location and a certain number of years of experience in any given industry.

But for authors, no such standardized guide exists. And looking across our industry isn't much help either, because while we have all heard of authors making six and seven figures a year from their work, I would venture a guess that for every one of those people, there are tens of thousands of others who do not yet even make a full-time living with their words. Therefore, those six-and-seven-figure folks *obviously* do not represent most of our industry.

Having said that, it *is* possible to assign your time a value—and quite frankly, you can use whatever number you want. The keys are to:

(a) realize that to more accurately record and then recoup that value, the 'clock' needs to start when you begin a new work and stop when that book is published, and to

(b) understand that it will take more sales of each book to reach break-even point when your time is factored into the costs to publish.

As an example, let's say that I assign a value to my time of $20 per hour. And let's say I spent four hours a day for sixty days to write *List of Secrets*. That comes to:

$20 per hour x 4 hours per day = $80 per day

$80 per day x 60 days = $4,800 worth of my time spent on writing *List of Secrets*.

Let's grab the data that we used back in Chapter Five to calculate break-even point for my e-book version of *List of Secrets*, and add in the cost of my time:

My fixed direct costs were $505.75 for the e-book format, and another $125.39 in indirect costs allocated to that title, for a total of $631.14.

Adding in my time, that goes up to $5,431.14 to publish *List of Secrets* as an e-book.

So now, my break-even calculation would look like this:

Break-Even Units = $5,431.14 / $3.49
Break-Even Units = 1,556

Basically, 1,556 units need to sell to break even *if* I keep my current pricing structure, which is $4.99 USD. (While

I could raise the price if I wanted to, $4.99 USD for that book's length and genre is appropriate.)

This is still very do-able, it will just take longer to get there. The good news is, once *List* was completed, my 'clock' stopped on that book, and reset for the next one.

***

Another arena in which you really do need to consider your value is with regard to contracts, and as Mark has many more years' expertise under his belt on this topic than I do, I'm climbing out from behind the wheel so he can give you all the good stuff you need to know about contracts.

***

Understanding the Costs and Benefits of Contracts

MLL

This book is written mostly from the point of view that you're an author who has come to the business of writing and publishing with an indie-author or self-publishing hat on.

Below I'm going to explain a few important things you need to consider when it comes to signing contracts with publishers.

However, as an indie author you need to know that when you self-publish, you are, indeed, signing a contract. Whether you publish direct to retail platforms (such as Kindle Direct Publishing, or Kobo Writing Life), or you use a third-party distributor (like Draft2Digital or Street-Lib), you are signing a contract.

I'm pretty sure that you, like 95% of authors out there, never even bothered to read-through the details of the contract. If anything, the key thing you likely attended to was how much money you would get in "royalties" for the sales of your books, and then glossed over everything else.

When I was creating Kobo Writing Life, I had to read through all the contracts being offered in order to generate, in collaboration with Kobo's legal team, a contract for use within that direct publishing platform. So I read them all.

In a nutshell, here are the high-level things you're agreeing to in the contracts for most of the major retail platforms (Amazon, Apple, Google Play, Kobo, and Nook) for eBook sales.

- You, as the owner of the IP in question, confirm that you have the legal rights to sell the book(s) in question in the territories they operate within.
- You are not giving up any of your rights or IP to this book and are free to also publish and sell it anywhere else (*see below for an important caveat related to this*)*
- You are allowing the retailer to sell, to their consumers, the products you are offering for an agreed-upon value they determine which is usually based upon the book's retail price.
- You can set the retail price (sometimes with restrictions on price ranges that may affect the "royalty" rate you are paid for those sales.
- You can remove (unpublish/delist) those books from retail sale under your own control at any time.
- You allow the retailer the ability to host your book in their cloud-based service so that those who purchase your books may have access to them even after you remove them from retail sale.
- The retailer can choose, at their own discretion, at any time, and for any reason of their

choosing, whether or not they will accept what you attempt to publish (*It is, after all, **their** retail store and they can decide what they want to sell and feature/promote on their digital retail shelves and to their customers. If you believe their unwillingness to sell certain types of books constitutes censorship, you truly don't understand the difference between censorship and a free and open market based on capitalism*)

- VERY IMPORTANT FOR eBOOKS (Because so many authors do not understand this): You **must not** sell the eBook at a lower retail price on any other online/retail platform (including your own website for direct sales). If you do, the retailer retains full rights to price-match at **your** cost.

* One important caveat to the 2nd of the 8 bullet points just listed is related to KDP Select. KDP Select is a free 90-day program for Kindle eBooks. It comes with the opportunity to reach a unique set of Kindle customers by making the book available in Kindle Unlimited, *a subscription program that allows readers to consume as many books as they wish for a monthly fee. Authors have access to a shared KDP Select Global Fund for additional revenue based on page reads, and limited Kindle Countdown Deal and Free Book Promotion options.*

If you enroll an eBook in KDP Select, the terms of that condition lock the book in for a 90-day exclusivity period that will automatically re-enroll by default. During this period, your eBook must be exclusive to Amazon Kindle, and you cannot be available for sale or even as a free give-away elsewhere, including on your own website.

Thus, though you still own the IP/rights to that book, the KDP Select terms prevent you from the freedom to publish it or license it elsewhere. You are, in effect, giving up that particular right. The good news is that, unlike many publishing contracts, the terms of the deal are only for 90 days. Also, this is a personal choice that **you** the author, can make, and revise, at any time. For example, if you're pulling in vast amounts of money via *Kindle Unlimited* page reads and it's working for you, you recognize the pros and cons of this contract clause.

That covers a very high-level look at the contracts you are signing when you self-publish a book. But what about publishing contracts? And how do they relate to the way you value the worth of your writing?

***

<u>Publishing Contracts</u>

One dream that many writers have—yes, even writers who have been killing it with digital indie publishing and are pulling in six and seven figure annual incomes from the sales of their eBooks—is signing a contract with a publisher.

The belief is that having a publisher means the writer will *not* have to do any marketing.

Please note that this is a misunderstanding.

While a publisher may do some of the marketing and may even assign an internal publicist to your book in the month prior to and the month of your book's release, that publicist is likely overseeing a dozen or more other authors and titles at the same time.

The reality is that, unless you signed with a major publisher for a significant advance (at least six, or perhaps seven figures), the marketing support you'll be getting is going to be minimal.

But there is value that comes with signing a publishing contract with a traditional publisher. And that plays right into the costs, like the details D.F. shared in *Chapter 4*.

I'll get to that below. But I first need you to understand one very significant aspect about publishing. In a traditional publishing contract ALL money should from the publisher to the author. If the author has to pay the publisher, or an editor, or a cover designer, or any other book-production aspect, this is a vanity publisher and **not** a real publisher. (Please see *Appendix A* for details on how to determine if a publisher is a real publisher or a vanity publishing services provider masquerading as a publisher)

Simply put, what a publishing contract ultimately represents is the belief of the publisher, that your book (your IP) that you are licensing to them for specified terms and compensation, is going to earn them enough revenues to profit from.

It is, in other words, that publisher's investment in you and your book(s). The publisher is ultimately responsible for production and distribution and some marketing costs.

But just because the publisher is investing in the production and distribution of your book doesn't mean that there aren't costs to you that you need to track. There are costs; they are just different from the costs of an indie author. Similarly, the income structure for traditionally published authors is different.

COSTS

In a traditional publishing scenario, the publisher is responsible for all the costs of production. This includes editing, layout, cover design, and distribution. But you should track and record the costs to you as an author in the creation of the book you have licensed to them through a contract.

And in most cases in the US and Canada, you can track these costs as part of your income tax even if you haven't yet signed a deal with a publisher yet. The key is that you can demonstrate, through your business activities, that there is a reasonable expectation of income.

Here are just some of the costs to consider:

- Paper, printer ink, stationary, envelopes
- The amortized cost of your printer, your computer, and other hardware used in your writing operations
- Postage, packaging, and shipping

- Research (books, articles, magazines, sub-scriptions) related to your writing
- Travel (for research)
- Travel (for conferences, workshops, seminars)
- Travel (for selling your books)
- Marketing—this can include postage for shipping review copies, reader giveaways, digital ads, digital and printed promotional material and assets

* As always, we highly recommend that you solicit the counsel and services of a professional accountant in your country/state/province to advise on where and how these costs can be applied on your income tax.

<u>AUTHOR INCOME</u>

When deciding to offer a contract to you, the publisher usually first has a belief that there is market demand for your book and is determining how much they will spend on you and this book to earn an overall net profit on it.

Your author income is paid in two different ways: An advance, and royalties.

An advance is the money that a publisher is willing to offer to you to lock in or contract you for the licensing of the rights of that book. It exists with the belief that the book will earn a lot more than the advance being offered, and the advance is the indication of the publisher's calculation that this book was a good business investment.

Advances are often paid in three installments.

- **1st Installment**—upon signing the contract
- **2nd Installment**—upon delivery of the manuscript
- **3rd Installment**—upon publication

Royalties are calculated from the publication date forward and represent a % of the selling price of the book.

Before royalties are paid to an author, they have to be 'earned out'. Once the accumulated royalties are greater than the total of the author's advance payment, the publisher starts paying the author those royalties.

Unlike in self-publishing, where authors are typically paid monthly, and often 45 to 90 days after the month where the sales are earned, traditional publishers often pay authors once or twice a year. In addition, most traditional publishers will include a 30% hold-back against potential returns.

Within traditional publishing and bookselling, bookstores can return books to a publisher up to 9 months after they acquired the book for stock in their stores. This means that, with the sale of any book comes the potential risk that bookstores might return unsold stock back to the publisher.

Publisher withhold 30% of their royalty payments to authors almost like an insurance payment against the costs of returns.

This means that for every $100 owed to an author, the publisher only pays the author $70 and holds back that additional $30 for a full year.

To illustrate, let me walk through the specific details of one of my own traditionally published books.

Traditional Publishing Book Example

In order to illustrate, via example, what the numbers might look like for a traditional publishing contract—particularly in relation to the indie publishing experience—let's walk through a real-life example of a book, the contract terms associated with it, the resulting sales, and what that means in terms of author income.

Book Title: Marky Mark & The Funky Book
Author: Mark Leslie
Publisher: Good Vibrations Publishing
Print Retail Price: $24.99
eBook Retail Price: $12.99

(*These details are actual numbers, but the name of the book and the name of the publisher are fictional*)

My contract for **Marky Mark & The Funky Book** came with an offer of an advance and royalties that range between 8% to 10%. (*I'll explain a little later why I might sign such a deal when we live in a world where I can earn 70% on eBook sales*).

Here are the main terms from the **AUTHOR COMPENSATION** portion of the 16-page contract.

Advance Against Royalties. The Publisher shall pay to the Author, as an advance against royalties and any other amounts owing by the Publisher to the Author under this Agreement, the sum of ONE THOUSAND dollars ($1000.00) to be paid as follows

- One-third upon signing of this Agreement (payment due within 30 days of signing)
- One-third upon delivery and acceptance of the complete Manuscript (acceptance shall mean editorial changes have been approved by the Author and rewriters undertaken by the Author have been approved by the Publisher)*
- One-third upon publication of the Work in the first Publisher's edition. For greater clarity, "Publication Date" shall mean sixty (60) days after the work is received in the Publisher's distribution warehouse.

Note that this technically isn't when the manuscript is first delivered, but only after it goes through multiple months of editorial passes, revisions, and a final proofread.

Royalties on the Publisher's Edition. For each Edition of the Work published by the Publisher under this Agreement, the Publisher shall credit the Author's account with the following royalties on Net Copies Sold:

- 8% of the List Price on all Net Copies Sold of any Print Editions
- 15% of Net Revenues from all sales of the Work in the Publisher's eBook format.
- "Print Edition" as used in this Agreement, refers to the Work as published in any particular length and format in print. If the Work is redesigned in any manner, then

the Work as revised shall be considered a new "Edition" for purposes of this Clause
- "Net Copies Sold" as used in this Agreement, means the sale less returns of any and all copies sold by the Publisher through conventional channels of distribution in the book trade, and does not include promotional and review copies, the Author's free copies, or copies for which a royalty rate is otherwise set forth in this Agreement
- "Net Revenues" as used in the Clause above, refers to the money actually received by the Publisher for the sale of eBook copies of the Work after deduction of fees and commissions, currency exchange discounts, and costs of collection, for greater certainty, not including revenues from sub-licensing

Reduced Royalties on the Publisher's Editions. For any and all sales of the Work in any Publisher's edition at discounts greater than 51% for wholesale discounts in the book trade; non-returnable sales; direct sales; export sales; and bulk, premium, and other special sales; the Author's royalty shall be 10% of net amount received. Sales of the Work in any category for which a reduced royalty is paid shall be excluded from the calculation of total sales for the purpose of determining the escalation of royalties.

There's another full page in the contract outlining the 50/50 share for subsidiary rights that the contract covers; this is basically, if the publisher sub-licenses foreign language rights, other formats, etc., the publisher and the author share those funds with a 50% split. (The publisher, in essence, acts like an agent, but with a much higher cut than the typically 15% an agent keeps). But for the sake of simplicity, I'll leave that out.

Let's walk through this real-life example using actual data.

The advance is paid out in installments of $333.33 over the course of anywhere from 6 months to 2 years. And, for print book sales, the earnings are $1.9992 per unit sold.

Here's a look at the annual royalty statement from the publisher (slightly simplified).

Royalty Details	Rate	Quantity	Amount
Trade—gross units sold		1,854	
Trade – return units		-368	
Trade – net units sold		1,486	
Reduced royalty units sold	51%	185	$2,307.45
eBooks units sold		65	$525.35
Full royalty at list price	8%		$2970.81
Reduced royalty (net revenue)	10%		$230.75
eBook royalty	15%		$78.80
Total royalty			$3,280.36
Royalty advance			-$1000.00
Current holdback	30%		-$984.11
Royalties earned			$1,296.25

To explain how this works, here's a breakdown.

The publisher calculates all sales and returns in the first year of the book's release to determine the net units sold via the regular trade market.

Then the publisher calculates the sales at reduced royalties (through special markets, etc.) where the royalties are significantly reduced and the eBook sales. (*You'll notice that this publisher, like many traditional publishers are more invested in selling print products over eBooks, direct most of their marketing on print, and over-price their eBooks, so eBook sales are almost laughable*).

Then the publisher totals the earnings from those three buckets to determine a total royalty for that period.

And from that they subtract the royalty advance amount. (*In this case, this book earned-out its royalty. At a rate of approximately $2.00 per unit sold, the book needs to sell 500 units to earn out that advance. Thus, only the sales quantity beyond the first 500 units will earn the author an actual income. From my experience, only one of my traditionally published titles did not earn out its advance in the first year. But I realize I'm rather lucky because most books published never earn back their advance.*)

The publisher also holds-back 30% of the royalty amount to buffer against future returns. That holdback amount will be paid in the following year.

***

WHY SIGN A TRADITIONAL CONTRACT?

It's pretty clear to see that, with traditional publishing there are a lot more "fingers in the pie" before the author sees any money for sales of that book.

In a nutshell here's how it breaks down:

If I license my IP to a traditional publisher, I can expect to earn $2.00 per print unit sold that I get paid for once a year with 30% withheld. (Which means I earn about $1.40 that first year and then the remaining $0.60 the next).

However, if I self-publish that book, I may earn anywhere between $1.00 to $4.00 on the POD/print book sales (the margin, because it represents multiple "fingers in the pie" is similarly small). But print book sales for most indie authors are inversely proportional to the eBook sales for a traditional publisher. It's on the eBook sales where I earn 70%. Meaning a book that retails for $4.99 earns me $3.49 that gets paid out monthly anywhere between 45 to 90 days after the sale.

So, what is the benefit of a traditional publishing contract for the average author? (*By average author, I mean the tens of thousands of authors who are **not** household names. I'm not talking about the mega-deals that authors like Stephen King, Nora Roberts, or James Patterson sign where the advances are significantly higher and the royalty rates, while they are nowhere near self-publishing rates, are still higher*).

I would argue that the benefit, apart from having someone else find and hire all the professionals needed, is access to the *old boys'* network of traditional publishing and distribution.

I have walked into bookstores in both Canada and the United States and been able to find one or more of my traditionally published books on the shelves for sale. One might call *that* vanity publishing. Because, while it feels good, it's rare that the satisfaction of seeing a book on bookstore shelves will come with the same sort of monetary compensation available to an indie author selling eBooks.

And, outside of traditional bookstores, one of my publishers has been able to get a few of my books into retailers such as Costco and Walmart. While that came with a decent sales volume lift, it certainly fed my ego a lot better than it fed my pocketbook.

Signing a traditional publishing contract might also come, for some authors, with a degree of personal pride and prestige. After all, a publisher deciding to invest their money, time, and energy into your book can come with a powerful sense of having "made it" as an author.

Besides these elements, there is a unique discoverability related to print books that doesn't happen in the same way with eBooks. If someone buys one of my eBooks from Amazon, Barnes & Noble, or Kobo, it sits "hidden" on their Kindle, Nook, or Kobo device. It's not visible to others. But a print copy is a physical advertisement in and of itself.

Considering the reality that most people who read still read print books, the discoverability of an author because of a physical item is still extremely powerful. Yes, I know, particularly if you're an indie author, and a successful indie author, you might have trouble believing just how small the overall readership is for eBooks. Yes, it's millions and millions of people who do read eBooks, enough to make five, six, and seven-figure authors out of hundreds of indie authors. But just imagine how many more readers still haven't adopted eBooks into their reading diets. (For me, I see this as an optimistic sign that indie authors have still only seen the very beginning of the eBook revolution. There are still millions more readers to discover this realm, and you and your books).

Because most traditional publishers are significantly better at print book sales and distribution, whenever I'm considering whether a book I'm writing should be indie published, or offered to a traditional publisher, I also consider how much a reader might prefer having the print book over the eBook.

Certain genres, for example, sell significantly better in print than in eBook. Juvenile and picture books, poetry, cookbooks, workbooks, non-fiction self-help and how-to books, are examples of books that typically sell far better in print than in eBook.

In my case, most of my "true ghost story" books that are based on specific locations (*Haunted Hamilton, Spooky Sudbury, Creepy Capital, Haunted Hospitals*) are books that people usually prefer to have physical copies of. They might be souvenirs of a visit to a particular city or location. *Tomes of Terror: Haunted Bookstores and Libraries* is carried by many of the bookstores and libraries that are featured in it.

Thus, when I'm deciding whether to offer a book to a more traditional publisher, I consider this factor of the physical product game. Yes, I'm giving up earning potential, and I'm signing over rights I'd rather maintain, but, like an author who chooses to be exclusive to Amazon Kindle to reap the benefits of *Kindle Unlimited* page reads, I'm making a calculated decision and weighing the pros and cons against my goals.

If I had my way—and this is something I truly hope the industry catches up with eventually—I'd much prefer to license my print book rights to a traditional publisher while maintaining my eBook, and perhaps my audiobook rights for publishing myself. That way I could ultimately optimize my earning potential.

Our industry, sadly, hasn't caught up to that. But I remain hopeful.

In the meantime, I recognize what I'm giving up on and what I'm gaining when I decide to sign a traditional publishing contract. It's a conscious and purposeful decision. It's not something I'm being tricked into, but rather something I have considered at length and made a very clear and determined decision about.

And so, if you are in the process of deciding if you should sign a contract with a traditional publisher, the next segment of this chapter will explore clauses that you might want to be careful of.

CONTRACT CLAUSES TO CONSIDER

Publishing contracts can be wieldy. As I mentioned earlier in this chapter, one of my contracts was 16 pages long. But if you only remember one thing about publishing contracts, remember this: a contract is a negotiation tool and thus can be changed. Let me repeat that.

A contract is a negotiation and thus can be changed.

Most publishers offer a boilerplate contract that is designed as a catch-all "rights-grab" to take control of and leverage as much of your IP as possible. No, they're not doing it out of evil intent or malice; they are merely offering a business deal and wish to make that deal preferable for themselves.

However, they'll often change the default terms of their boilerplate contract offer when requested.

The key, then, is requesting those changes.

You just have to ask.

For in depth details and advice, a book I highly recommend is Kristine Kathryn Rusch's 2016 book **Closing the Deal...on Your Terms:** *Agents, Contracts and Other Considerations.*

However, without getting into specifics of contract negotiation, or going into too much detail, here are some ideas of the different things you can request changes to:

- The advance amount—*Advances for the average author are dramatically lower than ever before; especially in the past decade or two. They typically start in the $500 to $1000 realm for most first-time authors.*
- The royalty percent—*Unless you are a big-name author, you're most likely going to be getting an offer of 8%. You might be able to get as high as 12 to 15% or 20% but that usually comes with a proven track record.*

- Reversion of rights clauses.
- Right of first refusal.
- Competition clauses (that may prevent you from selling to another publisher or self publishing).
- Kill-fees.
- Cost of author copies.
- Audiobook rights.
- eBook rights.
- Other non-book related rights.

Not every publisher you are in contract with is going to be amenable to changing the items listed above. Some might be flexible on one item, but not at all flexible on another.

But the key thing for you to remember is that a contract is a negotiation, and if you don't ask you definitely don't receive.

So, when you're comfortable giving up (or licensing some of your IP to a publisher), you should also be prepared to ask for changes to make that compromise worthwhile to you.

CHAPTER TEN:
Organization is Key

DFH

Part of record-keeping for your business should be organization; not just the assimilation of documents and receipts, but in how you approach your tracking of money flowing to and away from you—both present, and historically.

And the concept of organization goes together with record retention. After all, if you don't *need* to keep receipts forever, why would you?

For me personally, I take what my country's governing tax authority recommends, and I add two years, just to be safe. But I don't keep the historical in paper form. It gets scanned in and saved to a flash drive. I do mine this way for several reasons:

1) Less paper = less clutter taking up physical space
2) Flash drives cannot be hacked, like online 'storage' can
3) It's much simpler come tax return time to hand my CPA a flash drive than an unwieldy stack of crumpled receipts

Using this method enables me to hold onto several years' worth of data in the same amount of physical space that my cell phone would take up. Not too shabby.

Documents and receipts aside, let's talk organization *within your bookkeeping* for a moment. It just makes sense—not to mention, more simplified come tax season—to classify certain expenses together in a group. As an example: cover design, editing costs, and narration costs are all Costs of Goods Sold (COGS).

Some main expense categories to consider using in your author business are:

-   COGS (covers, editing, narration, translation, ISBN, etc.)
-   Dues & Subscriptions
-   Professional & Legal (copyright fees, for example)
-   Travel
-   Computer / Software
-   Marketing
-   Training & Development
-   Supplies
-   Postage / Shipping
-   Bank & Credit Card Fees

It's also important to abide by your state/provincial and federal income tax classifications. Ensuring you have mapped your expenses to the actual categories required in your annual tax forms is important so that, at the end of the year, you're not struggling to see where each expense might fit in.

Of course, organization really needs to go a step further than just tracking your income and expenses—and this is something that we'll explore even further in Chapter Eleven, but for now we'll pause and look at a different sort of long-term planning. Estate planning for authors.

CHAPTER ELEVEN
Estate Planning for Authors

MLL

One of the greatest things about being an indie author is that you're in complete control of your writing business. You get to decide the actions—you get to call the shots.

Even if you have a team that works with you—an assistant (virtual or otherwise), an accountant, editors, designers, marketing, and PR folks—often, most of your work is a solo endeavor.

So, what happens when you die?

No, I'm not trying to be morose; but let's face it, it's inevitable and will happen.

A Will is a document that states who gets what after you die.

But is that enough, particularly considering the value of your published works, not to mention all the associated IP you're leaving behind? Your IP has value that can last for another 70 years after your death.

My good friend M.L. (Matt) Buchman, who found himself earning the kind of living as an author to fully support his family, came to the startling realization that neither his wife, nor his daughter would know what to do with the writing business he had built up.

So, he wrote a letter to them. A final letter. Or, as Matt calls it, The Final Letter.

It's a letter that tells your heir(s) the ways to maintain the income-earning potential of your IP in the event of your death.

In 2017 he compiled details about this process into a book entitled **Estate Planning for Authors:** *Your Final Letter (and why you need to write it now)*. While this chapter summarizes a few of the important things Matt covers in the book, I highly recommend that you buy and read the book.

There are numerous cases where artists didn't properly indicate how their IP should be handled. This not only left their loved ones confused, in the dark, and often without the ability to understand what to do with their legacy, but it also often led to the misuse and loss of the power of their IP.

Here are some highlights of just a few examples:

- Jane Austin died in 1817 and by 1822 all her novels went out of print. Her heirs allowed that to happen. In 1832 a publisher purchased her copyright for 250 pounds (worth about £29,800 or just under $40,000 USD in today's money).
- Allen Drury, the author of the 1960 #1 New York Times Bestselling novel *Advise and Consent*, which also won the Pulitzer Prize. He died in 1998, and by 2013, not only was *Advise and Consent* the 27th most

sought after out-of-print book in the United States, but his heirs were living in poverty.

These are just a couple of examples of writers who either didn't leave clear instructions for the handling of their IP, or who neglected to understand the impact that not planning could have on. You are likely also familiar with what happens when artists (such as Prince, Elvis, or Aretha Franklin) either don't even have a will or neglect to leave explicit instructions on how to handle the creative IP of their estates and legacies.

You and your IP has worth that can provide for your heirs and loved ones long after you are gone.

Philip K. Dick, the award-winning science-fiction author of more than 44 novels and 121 short stories, died in March 1982, four months before the release of the Harrison Ford/Ridley Scott version of *Blade Runner*. Well over a dozen other movie and television adaptations were produced from his writing, including *Total Recall* (1990 and 2012), *Minority Report* (2002), *A Scanner Darkly* (2006), *The Adjustment Bureau* (2011), *Radio Free Albemuth* (2010) and *The Man in the High Castle* (2015 to 2019).

It can happen. So why would you leave any of what you have built as an author to chance?

So, get Matt's book, and read it.

I also highly recommend you don't delay and at least get started on that letter, and the corresponding documents, as soon as possible.

While I read the book back in 2017 and had long discussions with Matt about the process (*I even interviewed him about it for Episode 92 of the Stark Reflections on Writing and Publishing Podcast in August 2019*) I still didn't get around to writing that letter.

Not until March 2021. I was scheduled to go in for an overdue hernia surgery on March 16, 2021. And I had a really bad feeling leading up to that date.

Part of that feeling naturally came because on March 17, 2003, my dad went in for surgery. He died in the recovery room when the clips on his renal artery came out and he bled to death. He was a gregarious and positive man; he loved to tell jokes, make people laugh, and put them at ease. He was rarely negative in his outlook. But prior to that surgery he mentioned he had a bad feeling about it.

I decided not to ignore my own bad feeling.

And while I didn't want to put off or cancel the surgery—the pain I experienced from the hernia was getting to be unbearable—I did two things.

I convinced the anesthesiologist and surgeon, the day of my surgery, to allow me to remain awake for the operation (for some reason my fear wasn't in the operation itself, but in being put right out), and I finally prepared my own Final Letter for my partner Liz.

In fact, as I type this, I can reach over to where this large brown 8 X 10 envelope is tucked into the bookshelves to my right in my home office.

It reads:

LIZ
IF MARK, YOU KNOW....
XOXO

This package contains many of the things outlined in Matt's book, as well as a personal letter to both Liz and my son Alexander.

You see, while Liz is supportive of my writing and we talk about it all the time, she has absolutely no idea about the logistics of my operation. Sure, there are contracts for the traditionally published books of mine, and in most cases, the publisher will continue to send checks for royalties.

But what about the books I have self-published? What platforms am I using to get to the numerous retailers and libraries where my books are available? What ads might I be running that are ongoing? What future promotions and commitments have I locked myself into that she would be unaware of? And where can she find any of that information within the filing cabinets, my computers, and in the cloud folders out there?

Yikes!

While Matt's book outlines this in far more detail, D.F. and I thought it would be best to review the basics and remind you of just some of the things that are important for planning your estate for the long haul for your heirs.

Your Final Letter should be a clear statement of your desires on how you would like your heir(s) to handle your overall IP along with detailed instructions on where and how they will be able to access your accounts and files, both physical and digital.

And your heir(s) might decide to manage the estate by themselves, hire a fee-based service to assist, hire an author or publisher to assist, sell it off, or give/donate it to a cause.

Whatever they decide, it will, at least, be informed by your desires and your careful explanation of this business of writing and publishing.

In summary, here's what you should consider:

Clearly Explain in Non-Writer-Speak English

When I'm speaking with fellow writers, I can throw out terms and abbreviations without a second thought. But would your heir(s) know what KDP, KU or even ISBN mean?

It might make sense to either craft (or copy and paste from trusted resources) a very high-level glossary of terms that you'll be using in your instructions.

Consider a Trusted Author Insider Colleague

While your heir(s) may inherit your IP, there are likely people you have worked with (in person or virtual) that know the business and can be trusted. You may want to suggest to your heir(s) that one or more particular people are trusted friends who can help explain complicated elements of the business of writing and publishing.

Just make sure you've given those friends/colleagues a heads up that, should anything happen to you, they might be contacted for support/help with understanding or explaining *authorly* things.

Make a Checklist/Outline of all the Elements

Regardless of whether you outline as a writer, prior to creating Your Final Letter, it will be handy to outline the various elements that will be covered:

- Introduction
- Where can I find all the key stuff?
- Passwords, logins, account information
- What content is kept where? The master files for your contracts/legal agreements. The master files for your book assets themselves
- The names and contact info of one or more trusted colleagues for support/help or to answer questions
- A glossary or helpful explanation of the vocabulary of your writing/publishing business
- The money details. Banks, accounts, funds, investments. Don't forget subscriptions and advertising accounts
- Conclusion/Sign off

It is also a good idea to have a discussion with your heir(s) prior to putting together the package. Make sure they are familiar with where to find the master document. Also, if you have a backup that is stored, perhaps, in a safe deposit box, or in some digital format, ensure that they have access to it.

No, it's not an easy or a comfortable conversation.

When I tried to explain to Liz what I put into that large 8 X 10 envelope and why, she initially didn't want to have any of that talk. But we had the talk, and she knows where that envelope is.

I should, of course, revisit that envelope and update it, because, since I initially wrote it, there are new accounts I've created, new contracts I've signed, and updated details to add.

Because, remember, that final letter should be a living and dynamic document that you should revisit perhaps once every year—maybe even during income tax season since that's another annual event necessary for the ongoing success of your business.

CHAPTER TWELVE:
Tools to Help You

DFH

<u>Cost-Saving Tips and Tricks</u>

Now let's talk for a minute about the 'must-have's' to be an author…which makes me roll my eyes. Seriously.

What to Write With

If you have the means to type words on a page, you're already well on your way. Some people swear by specialized writing software like Scrivener. I'm here to tell you that you do not *have* to put money out for things like that to get a book written—unless you just want to.

I've written seventeen books as of January 2022, and I've done every single one of them using Microsoft Word—a program that was already on my computer.

If you already have Word (or the Mac equivalent) on your computer, and especially if you're already comfortable with it, why not start there? Word has some good built-in features such as 'read-aloud', which can help you catch things that Grammarly or a spell-check program might not, like transposed words.

This is where I remind you again to play to your strengths and look past the "money factor" to also take your *time budget* under advisement. A lot of the specialized writing programs have cool bells and whistles, it's true. They also have a learning curve, so, keep that in mind.

You are, of course, welcome to use whatever you like to help you capture your brilliance into a story that readers can devour. Just be leery of anyone who says 'you *have to* use X program to get this book writing stuff done' — because no, you really don't. Not even Word.

Covers

Covers. So important for us to make sure that we've captured the right energy, the right imagery, to lure in our future super-fans.

But what about those of us who can't (or don't want to) spend a thousand dollars on a single cover?

My recommendation? Research your targeted genre, find out who some designers are that build covers for that genre, check out their websites, and ask about "pre-made" covers. For a fraction of the cost of a 'build from scratch' cover, a lot of designers have a gallery of pre-made covers they can tweak with your book's information.

If you're worried about 'pre-mades' not being high-enough quality for your work, go check out my *Vital*

Secrets series covers. Every single one of them was a pre-made that my designer made small modifications to.

***

Record-Keeping and Organization

Here are some things that can help you along the way to keep your records efficiently and better understand your business; after all, your report build results will only be as good as the data that comprises them, so you need to make sure that you've captured all the pieces correctly.

Getting your Sales Data

For those in the audience who are exclusive to a single retailer, it is easier to track your sales. After all, you're only pulling data from one storefront. But for those who are 'wide', that is, who publish their books to multiple storefronts, it can be more of a hassle unless you use a data aggregator to harvest your information for you.

I have personally used three different data aggregators to date in my author career: BookTrakr, BookReport, and ScribeCount. Information on each is listed below, along with pricing and pros and cons so that you can make an educated decision on which will work best for you and your situation.

BookTrakr

This aggregator pulls data from multiple storefronts and presents your data in an easy-to-follow format. The dashboard presents you with a summary of data, but also breaks out each book's activity for you. Other tabs show sales, reviews, and rankings, depending on if you have a Basic or Pro subscription.

BookTrakr bills monthly, and their pricing is based on the number of SKU's your catalogue has (number of books x number of places the books are sold). For example, if you have three e-books that you publish to four stores, that's a total of twelve SKU's. As of the writing of this chapter, its pricing structure is as follows:

# of SKUs	Monthly Cost		Yearly Cost	
	Basic	Pro	Basic	Pro
0-9	$0.99	$1.99	$10.99	$21.99
10-49	$4.99	$9.99	$54.99	$109.99
50-199	$9.99	$19.99	$109.99	$219.99
200-399	$19.99	$39.99	$219.99	$439.99
400-599	$29.99	$59.99	$329.99	$659.99
600-799	$39.99	$79.99	$439.99	$879.99
800-999	$49.99	$99.99	$549.99	$1,099.99

BookTrakr PROS: Pulls from more than one storefront, dashboard is easy to navigate, and they send you a daily summary email.

BookTrakr CONS: If you have a large catalogue and/or are a 'wide' author, this subscription can get expensive - and because their structure is based on SKU's and not sales, you are charged each month whether or not you make any sales. BookTrakr does not provide the ability to track expenses as well as sales. Also, they need your login information for each storefront to be able to retrieve your data for you.

BookReport

This aggregator connects into your KDP (Amazon) account and retrieves sales, ranking, and reviews data for you. Its dashboard is laid out nicely and easy to navigate.

BookReport's pricing is subscription-based, versus the SKU concept that BookTrakr uses.

BookReport PROS: Easy to navigate and easy to set up. Free to use until your KDP account earns more than $1,000 in a 30-day period, at which point you can either opt to pay $19 monthly or $190 annually.

BookReport CONS: If you publish to more than just Amazon you will need to pull the data from the other stores manually. BookReport only pulls your KDP data.

BookReport also does not provide the ability to track expenses as well as sales.

ScribeCount

ScribeCount is the latest player on the data aggregator market. Like BookTrakr, this aggregator pulls your data from multiple storefronts and presents the information in a super easy-to-navigate platform.

ScribeCount's pricing structure is subscription-based; however, unlike BookReport's structure, ScribeCount's is fluid and *moves up and down* along with your sales.

ScribeCount PROS: Data from multiple storefronts without having to hand over your login information, and robust reporting that includes the ability to enter your expenses and get a 'snapshot' of your net profit/loss at any given point in time. ScribeCount also lets you select your default currency; this means that you set it one time, and from then on, all data pulled into your ScribeCount account will be *automatically converted* to your default currency for you.

ScribeCount's budget-friendly pricing structure slides up or down to mirror your sales. This sliding mimics the storefronts' typical spacing between when a sale is made and when it is funded, which is on average sixty days. As an example, for March, your monthly cost would be based upon January sales.

As of the writing of this chapter, ScribeCount's monthly pricing structure is:

- FREE if your prior (sixty-day) period's sales were under $1,000
- $15 if your prior (sixty-day) period's sales were between $1001 - $2000
- $20 if your prior (sixty-day) period's sales were $2001 and above

Optionally, you can choose to just pay an annual rate. Currently (Jan 2022) that rate is showing to be $185 after a discount.

ScribeCount CONS: Cannot be used with the Safari browser application yet, so if you are a Mac user, they recommend using Chrome as your browser.

All things considered - time, ease of use, customization, and cost—Both D.F.'s and Mark's "Bang for Buck" recommendation for data aggregator companies is ScribeCount.

***

Record Keeping - 'Do-It-Yourself' versus Hiring an Accountant or Bookkeeper

Two main questions typically come up when the topic of recordkeeping is discussed:

1) Should I use accounting software? And if so, what kind?
2) Should I hire an accountant to keep track of my sales and expenses? And if so, when - and what should I look for?

Let's look at the answers to each of those questions in detail.

Should I use accounting software? And if so, what kind?

I will tell you now that as far as your day-to-day tracking of revenue and expenses and your Income Statement goes, no accounting software is needed; building an income statement in Excel (or Numbers, if you're a Mac user) works wonderfully regardless of whether you've chosen the cash-basis or accrual-basis method.

In my mind, the bigger question to ask is: *does your time budget allow for the learning curve that's required for most accounting software?*

Not to mention that whether you are using a specialized software for your business, or are keeping track of it all in Excel, regularly scheduled data entry will *still* be a requirement. There's just no getting around that part— unless you hire someone to maintain your business's books for you.

If you're a do-it-yourself type who just needs some Excel spreadsheets to get you started, click here to get on my mailing list and get a couple of free templates that you can use.

If you feel you absolutely need to buy accounting software, the best cost-effective recommendation I can give for a package that does <u>not</u> take advanced accounting knowledge to learn is QuickBooks. And yes, they *do* have a version geared especially for folks outside the U.S. called Online Global, as well as online support. Start here to learn more about QuickBooks.

Should I hire an accountant to keep track of my sales and expenses? And if so, when and what should I look for?

If you opt to turn over the day-to-day bookkeeping chore to someone else, here are some general tips:

a) Don't be afraid to ask questions. Ask them their background. Ask them how many years of experience they have—and in what *type* of accounting environment. Guidelines for non-profit accounting are much different from governmental or public-sector accounting, and both of those differ from private-sector accounting. You're going to want to get someone who has hands-on experience with *private-sector* accounting. If they're already used to dealing with the particulars of an author's business, such as royalties paid up to ninety days after they're earned, so much the better.

b) Be clear with them from the start whether you want to use the cash-basis or accrual-basis method; as previously shown, it makes a substantial difference in the timing with which transactions are recorded.

c) Ideally, the bookkeeper or accountant you hire will have at least *some* familiarity with the tax rules & regulations in your jurisdiction. If they don't it isn't a deal-breaker; you just need to consider also using an actual CPA or certified tax professional in your jurisdiction to file your returns when the time comes to ensure they're done correctly. (A second or third pair of eyes reviewing your business's activity for accuracy is never a terrible thing.)

d) Regarding timing of when to make the move from 'do-it-yourself' to hiring someone. That's an individual decision. I would say take a step back and look at both your money *and* your time budgets to help answer that. You may find it's well worth the monetary spend of hiring a third party if it frees up a large chunk of your time to spend on other aspects of your author business.

CHAPTER THIRTEEN:
Introduction to Financial Reports

DFH

Before we get in to building financial reports, I need to repeat some very key information about accounting methodology.

As said previously, all accounting transactions are done via the **double-entry** process (balancing the see-saw).

A good real-world example is paying a bill. Let's say I bought a cover for $75. The cost of that cover I would record as a COGS expense. But I *also* need to lower the amount in my business's cash account by $75, because that $75 is not available for me to use any longer.

Now, as I mentioned earlier, if you use the **cash-basis method**, items are not recorded until *money changes hands*. Because nothing is registered until money moves, you can only record cash account-related transactions, i.e., cash, expense, and income. You cannot use this method to track long-term financial items or inventory. On your Balance Sheet and Income Statement you would only include those items for that period that have been funded — whether it's inbound (royalty payment) or outbound (cover designer).

And earlier I told you that in the **accrual-basis method**, transactions are recorded *when they happen, regardless of when the money changes hands*. Because so many more accounts are needed to track pending items, the accrual method is the more complex of the two methods. However, this method *does* allow for things like royalties owed to you that have not been paid out yet.

EXAMPLES:

1) I sell $200 worth of books in March.

In the *cash method*, I would not record those sales until the royalty payment for it is *paid to me*—so, not until anywhere from April to June.

In the *accrual method*, I would record those sales in March.

2) I receive a $500 bill for my annual membership to an author organization on December 15th, but the payment is not due until January 2nd.

In the *cash method*, I would record that bill when I *pay* it, so, January 2nd.

In the *accrual method*, I would record that bill on the day I *receive* the bill, so, December 15th.

Pros and Cons of the Cash Method

The cash method is simpler than the accrual method, it provides a better picture of real-time cashflow, and income is not subject to taxation until the money is received.

However, it can also present a misleading picture of your business's *long-term* financial health. And it also does not allow for inventory tracking—any paperback copies you buy for an upcoming signing event, for example, would simply be expensed out and not considered inventory.

Pros and Cons of the Accrual Method

The accrual method is much more complex than the cash method, as I will demonstrate here momentarily. Another disadvantage is that since money not actually received yet is included in your numbers, there could be income tax liability in the present for those future dollars received. But, since it *recognizes activity in the period in which it happens rather than when money changes hands*, the accrual method tends to present a more accurate picture of the company's overall health over a longer amount of time than the cash method does.

Examples of Each Method's Entries

If I am recording those $200 March sales we talked about, I can simply record them as sales and increase my bank account by that same amount when I receive that money if I am using the cash method.

In the accrual method, since that money isn't coming for up to three months, I would go ahead and record the sales, but instead of increasing my bank account (because I have not actually been paid yet) *I need to find a different account to put the second half of my entry in to balance the see-saw.* For that, the accrual method uses what I like to refer as to as 'placeholder' accounts. These are temporary holding accounts if you will. And once that money is received, I would move that amount out of the placeholder account and over to the cash account to complete the recording of those sales.

This is what each method's entry (or for accrual, entries) would look like if I had $200 in sales in March that paid out to me in June:

Cash Method
The entry:
June 2020
- Increase Sales Account $200
- Increase Cash Account $200

Accrual Method
The first entry:
March 2020
- Increase Sales Account $200
- Increase Receivables $200

The second entry:
June 2020
- Increase Cash Account $200
- Decrease Receivables $200

And let's also look at that cover I bought for $75. Let's say I got the bill from my designer on the third of April, but he has 30-day terms on his invoice, so, it wasn't due until May 3rd. Let's say that I paid it on the due date. Here's how that would look in each method:

Cash Method
The entry:
May 2020
- Increase COGS expense $75
- Decrease Cash Account $75

Accrual Method:
The first entry:
April 2020
- Increase COGS expense $75
- Increase Payables $75

The second entry:
May 2020
- Decrease Payables $75
- Decrease Cash Account $75

Which method to use is up to you—for the most part. For example, in the United States, publicly traded companies and those entities who have more than $26 million annually in sales are *required* to use the accrual-basis method, but typically, small businesses may choose either method, so long as they use that method consistently.

NOTE: It is possible to use one method for tax reporting and the other for financial reporting. **Check with your local professional for recommendations as to the best path for you.**

Regardless of whether you go with the cash-basis or accrual-basis method, if you use accounting software your financial report generation will happen automatically, and the software will automatically record / move things into their proper 'buckets' as you go. For example, in accounting software, expenses are typically entered through the Accounts Payable module of the system, so, the holding account selected, by default, is Payables. And when the bill is paid, the system will automatically decrease Payables and your Cash Account for you.

The same is true if you opt to let a third party manage your records; a bookkeeper or accountant will be able to accurately record your items for you, so long as you make clear to them exactly how you want your expense categories arranged (if you're confused by this, we talked about it in Chapter Ten: Organization Is Key).

If, however, you are a do-it-yourself type and you don't want to use accounting software, it is possible (and easy) to track your income and expenses in Excel and to at least build your Income Statement, especially if you opt to use the cash method since it is much more straightforward.

***

Important Notes about financial reporting

A couple of key things to keep in mind when getting into the reporting piece of things are:

1) **Income Statement data** _starts over again at zero each year; your net income/loss rolls over to the Retained_

Earnings line of your balance sheet at the end of every year. An Income Statement captures activity for a period (or periods) of time. **Balance Sheet data** is <u>cumulative</u> *over the life of your business* and reflects what's happening *on a specific date.*

2) **A word of caution**—if you don't let a pro handle your stuff, or at least use accounting software, then building your <u>balance sheet</u> can become complicated *if you are using the accrual method.* The reason for this is simply because you must *manually* move items in and out of those placeholder accounts in real time to maintain an accurate picture of what is going on. This can become very time intensive.

Having said that, I will walk you through the typical components of a balance sheet, with the disclaimer that (as many of my professional colleagues will attest) building a balance sheet manually without using any sort of accounting software when you're utilizing the accrual method can be a pain.

***

Financial Statement Building Resources

For those of you who want a blow-by-blow deeper dive into the world of financial statement building beyond what we're about to cover, I recommend Thomas Ittelson's *Financial Statements: A Step-by-Step Guide to Understanding and Creating Financial Reports.*

A couple of caveats:

1) Mr. Ittelson's approach is based upon US GAAP standards (Generally Accepted Accounting Principles) versus IFRS guidelines (International Financial Reporting Standards), so bear that in mind.

2) His book walks the reader through the world of financial report building via a fictional manufacturing company, so some things he covers will simply not apply to an author's business.

Link to Mr. Ittelson's book:
https://books2read.com/u/49kLnX

TIME TO TAKE ANOTHER DEEP BREATH

MLL

The chapter you are about to read contains balance sheets and income statements.

Please don't be frightened by those.

Just looking at a spreadsheet can send some of us into a tizzy. The idea of it can inspire nightmares. Heck, I was on a board of directors for a recently forming company and most of the board admitted they would rather quit the board altogether than to become Treasurer. Thank goodness that there are people like D.F. in the world who love balance sheets and income statements and all the associated details.

Just remember that, while this book is meant to help introduce you to and familiarize yourself with accounting principles as they relate to your author business, we don't expect every single reader to walk away from this book one hundred percent mastering accounting.

Heck, we'd be happy if you walk away a little less frightened of accounting and understanding a few key details.

That's why we offer pre-made spreadsheets of data for you to use as templates on this book's resource URL - and it is also why many authors may choose to understand the high-level concepts and how it works but end up hiring their own accounting professional with the actual implementation of the necessary tracking.

CHAPTER FOURTEEN:
Balance Sheet and Income Statement

DFH

Balance Sheet and **Income Statement** are the two most common types of financial reports.

The **Balance Sheet** is the 'show the math' version of the *Accounting Equation*, which learned about in Chapter Three.

The **Income Statement** is the 'show the math' version of your sales (*Revenue)* minus all your expenses (including *Cost of Sales*) and shows you your *Net Profit or Loss.*

Why do they exist and why should you use them?

Because looking at them can give you an overall picture of how well or how poorly your business is doing, and if you drill down into the pieces that form these reports, you often can spot problem areas or trends that need more attention.

In accounting, the 'one to rule them all' is a section called General Ledger. This is where all the activity from the Accounts Payable and Accounts Receivable and Inventory parts come together. It is the contents of the General Ledger that form the basis of your Balance Sheet and Income Statement.

To help facilitate this, there exists what is known as a Chart of Accounts—basically, a list of every category your business is using. And how and where they land on financial reports depends upon how you set them up.

The Chart of Accounts is the assignment of a series of numeric 'codes' that you can use to place Balance Sheet items on the Balance Sheet and Income Statement items on the Income Statement. They can be four-digit, five-digit, even twelve-digit. *The length of each numeric code is immaterial. What's important is the first number of each one.*

Accounts starting with:

- 1 = your ASSET accounts
- 2 = your LIABILITY accounts
- 3 = your EQUITY accounts
- 4 = your REVENUE accounts
- 5 = your COGS accounts
- 6, 7, 8, 9 = your G&A accounts

In plain English, your *balance sheet will consist of values from codes beginning with 1, 2, and 3,* while your *income statement will be comprised of the values of codes beginning with 4 through 9.*

Here's a look at a typical Chart of Accounts in which the first column is the GL Chart of Accounts number I assigned to each category, the second column is that category's description, and the last column reminds me where each account's balance will land on my reporting:

G/Lcode	Description	TYPE
11150	Cash-Operating	(1) Asset
11400	Cash-Petty Cash	(1) Asset
12000	Accounts Receivable	(1) Asset
12990	Allowance for Bad Debts	(1) Asset
14110	Inventory	(1) Asset
15704	Capital Expenditures	(1) Asset
15990	Prepaids	(1) Asset
16000	Building	(1) Asset
16100	Computer Equipment	(1) Asset
16200	Leasehold Improvements	(1) Asset
16300	Office Equipment	(1) Asset
16400	Plant Machinery & Equipment	(1) Asset
16500	Transportation Equipment	(1) Asset
16900	Accumulated Depreciation	(1) Asset
18100	Deposits	(1) Asset
18300	Copyright / Trademark	(1) Asset
21000	Accounts Payable	(2) Liability
21300	Sales Tax Payable	(2) Liability
21900	Federal Income Tax Payable	(2) Liability
23400	Accrued Professional & Legal	(2) Liability
24100	Accrued Other	(2) Liability
26000	N/P-Current Portion	(2) Liability
26300	Unearned Income	(2) Liability
27900	N/P - Current (negative from LDT)	(2) Liability
31000	Common Stock	(3) Equity
31300	Retained Earnings	(3) Equity
31400	S Corp Distributions	(3) Equity
41100	Revenue	(4) Income
51100	COGS	(8) Expense
60110	Advertising	(8) Expense
60120	Auto Expense	(8) Expense
60160	Delivery	(8) Expense
60240	Dues & Subscriptions	(8) Expense
60242	Equipment - Rent	(8) Expense
60270	Equipment - Repairs	(8) Expense
60280	Insurance - Property & Casualty	(8) Expense
60286	Insurance - Liability	(8) Expense
60287	Meals & Entertainment	(8) Expense
70100	Bad Debts	(8) Expense
80132	Bank & Card Fees	(8) Expense
80220	Computer/Software	(8) Expense
90110	Interest Expense	(8) Expense
90130	Other Income and Expenses	(8) Expense
90150	Interest Revenue	(8) Expense
90160	Gain (Loss) from Fixed Asset Disposition	(8) Expense
90190	Charitable Contributions	(8) Expense

***

Balance Sheet—Accrual Method

For most companies in most industries, a **balance sheet** will look something like the image below, which is based on the *accrual-basis* method:

ASSETS		
Current Assets		
Cash Accounts		
Accounts Receivable – Net		
Inventory		
Prepaid Expenses	$	–
Total Current Assets	$	–
Long-Term Assets		
Fixed Asset Value	$	–
Less Accumulated Depreciation	$	–
Net Fixed Assets	$	–
Other Assets (Deposits, IP, copyright, trademarks, customer lists)		
Deposits	$	–
IP (copyright, trademarks)	$	–
Less Accumulated Amortization of IP	$	–
Net Other Assets	$	–
Total Assets	**$**	**–**
LIABILITIES AND OWNERS' EQUITY		
Current Liabilities		
Current Portion of Long-Term Debt	$	–
Line of Credit	$	–
Accounts Payable		
Accrued Expenses	$	–
Unearned Income	$	–
Total Current Liabilities	$	–
Long-Term Debt		
Financial Institutions	$	–
Stockholders	$	–
Less Current Portion of Long-Term Debt	$	–
Net Long-Term Debt	$	–
Owners' Equity		
Common Stock	$	–
Retained Earnings		
Owner Distributions	$	–
Total Equity	$	–
Total Liabilties and Owners' Equity	**$**	**–**

But as I said, most companies use the *accrual-basis method* of recording their activity, so line items such as Accounts Receivable, Accounts Payable, Inventory, Accrued Expenses, and Prepaid Expenses are necessary to accurately reflect everything that is happening.

Here's what each line item involves:

Current Assets section:

"**Cash Accounts**" - Literally, your business checking and savings account balances.

"**Accounts Receivable - Net**" - simply means the total of any monies owed to you minus any reserves. For other businesses, 'reserves' consists of things like a bad debt allowance. For authors, 'reserves' would typically be things like putting back a percentage as a cushion to cover readers or stores returning your books for a refund.

"**Inventory**" - items produced for sale.

"**Prepaid Expenses**" - These are things typically paid in a lump-sum but that cover more than one accounting period.

Long-Term Assets section:

"**Fixed Asset Value**"—Won't be common for authors; this category will consist of things like buildings, land, and equipment. You can either expense the value all at once, or, you can log it as a fixed asset and then gradually record the change in value via depreciation.

"**Accumulated Depreciation**" - Correlates to "Fixed Assets". This is the amount of reduction of fixed asset value at any given point in time. (And if you do not have any fixed assets, you will not have any depreciation).

Other Assets section:

Trademarks, copyrights, and Intellectual Property goes here, as would any deposits you have paid out. (In other businesses it's typically security deposits.) Note that with intangible assets, we *gradually reduce the value over time* using amortization, just like we do with fixed assets and depreciation.

LIABILITIES section:

Current Liabilities—(due within a twelve-month period):

"**Current Portion of Long-Term Debt**" - If you have a multiple-year note or loan, you include the current year's portion of payments here. This is NOT common for authors.

"**Line of Credit**" - Only used to record any unsecured (i.e., NOT collateral based) lines of credit your business might have with a financial institution. This will NOT be common for authors.

"**Accounts Payable**" - Expenses you have received a bill for but have not paid yet.

"**Accrued Expenses**" - This helps you level out the one-off hits to your budget and your Income Statement. If you know you will have a big expense coming up every, say, March, you can put in a 'placeholder' entry for a portion of it each month, and then remove the accrual once that bill is received. (This would be an ideal place to record estimated taxes, hint, hint).

"**Unearned Income**" - If you have received an advance from a traditional publisher, it would be recorded under current liabilities on its own line; typically, it's called Unearned Income. An advance is considered a liability and not an asset, because it is income received before the 'work' has been performed, so a contractual obligation still exists to complete the work.

Long-Term Debt (past a twelve-month period). NONE of these will apply to most authors.

"**Financial Institutions**" are the payments owed on a note or loan.

"**Stockholders**" shouldn't come into play unless your company setup is an LLC or Corporation.

"**Less current portion of long-term debt**" shows the reduction of total notes/loans owed by the current year's portion of payments.

OWNER'S EQUITY section:

"**Common Stock**" will not apply to anyone but a corporation; this is referencing stock shares.

"**Retained Earnings**" is the *cumulative* Net Income/ Loss that a business keeps for future use. At the end of each financial period, net income/loss is reclassified to Retained Earnings.

"**Owner Distributions**" is simply that - monies paid out to the owner(s) over the course of time. These distributions reduce the amount of retained earnings that the business can use—which is why they will show up as a negative balance.

***

Balance Sheet—Cash Method

For the *cash-basis* crowd, the **balance sheet** becomes much more streamlined, as you will see in the image below. Remember, a cash-basis balance sheet will consist only of items where money has already changed hands. Because of that, a typical balance sheet for an author using the *cash-basis* method will consist of the following: the total of any of your business's **cash** (checking and/or savings) accounts, any **fixed assets**, any **unearned income** that you were paid, your **retained earnings**, and any **owner distributions** taken. *Cash-basis* method means there are no liabilities to record because everything's already been paid—unless you have been paid an advance:

BALANCE SHEET
Month / year   Month / year

ASSETS

<u>Current Assets</u>
     Cash Accounts

<u>Fixed Assets</u>
     Fixed Asset Value $ -
     Less Accumulated Depreciation $ -
       Net Fixed Assets $ -

Total Assets $ -

LIABILITIES AND OWNERS' EQUITY

<u>Current Liabilities</u>
     Unearned Income

<u>Owners' Equity</u>
     Retained Earnings
     Owner Distributions
Total Owner's Equity $ -

Total Liabilties and Owners' Equity $ -

***

Income Statement

The good news is that the **income statement** format stays constant, regardless of the accounting method used, and quite frankly, you will find the income statement to be the more useful to you on a regular basis.

The single difference between building an income statement for accrual-basis versus cash-basis lies *in the timing with which things are shown* on the statement.

Following are two Income Statements showing all sales as one line item and one group of COGS. One sheet is based on the accrual method and the other on the cash method.

Can you find where the difference in recording method appears?

INPUT YOUR DATA (per month $)	FYE Total
Income Statement - ACCRUAL BASIS	
Month's sales: (Enter TOTAL EARNED ALL places)	$ -
YTD Gross Income	$ -
EXPENSES: Enter monthly per category, if none, enter "0"	
COGS:	
Cover Design	$ -
Editing	$ -
Formatting	$ -
Barcodes/ISBN's	$ -
Narrations	$ -
Translations	$ -
	$ -
	$ -
	$ -
TOTAL COGS	$ -
G&A: Enter monthly per category, if none, enter "0"	
Newsletter Service provider	$ -
Software	$ -
Subscriber Build Services (Bookfunnel, StoryOrigin, Booksweeps,et	$ -
ScribeCount - Monthly	$ -
Dues & Subscriptions	$ -
Website	$ -
Office Supplies	$ -
Bank and CC fees	$ -
Accounting / Business OH expenses	$ -
Admin Asst	$ -
Marketing Spend (auto-fills from Marketing Tab)	$ -
G&A Total	$ -
TOTAL EXPENSE	$ -
Net Income Gain / (Loss)	$ -
Total Spend % of Sales	
Promo % of sales	$ -

	A	N
	INPUT YOUR DATA (per month $)	
	Income Statement - CASH BASIS	**FYE Total**
	Month's sales (When PAID)	
	YTD Gross Income	$ -
	EXPENSES:	
	COGS:	
	Cover Design	
)	Editing	
I	Formatting	
2	Barcodes/ISBN's	
3	Book Stock Order	
4		
5		
5		
7		
3	TOTAL COGS	
9	G&A:	
)	Mailchimp - Monthly	
I	Bookfunnel - Monthly	
2	Microsoft - Annual (renews Aug)	
3	ScribeCount - Monthly	
4	Story Origin - Annually	
5	Dues & Subs - ALLi, Patreon	
5	Wordpress - Annual (renews April)	
7	WooComm - Annual (renews Oct)	
3	CPA Fees / PA fees	
9	G SUITE - Annual - (renews Oct)	
)	Promo Spend (from Ad Spend Tab)	
I	TOTAL G&A	$ -
2	TOTAL EXPENSE	
3		
4	Net Income Gain / (Loss)	
5	Total Spend % of Sales	
5	Promo % of sales	$ -

The answer can be found in the first few rows.

The first example is accrual-based, so, income is recorded *as it is earned*, not when you're paid.

The second Excel is cash-based, so, only money you've *actually been paid* is being listed in the Gross Income section!

***

It's Okay to *Not* Dive Too Deep

MLL

I'm sticking my nose in for a moment here to remind you of something important.

D.F. is a professional accountant. An MBA. She is also a strategic and thorough planner. It's important for her, when writing a book on a topic related to what she has worked at professionally for decades, that she leaves nothing out.

Thus, the next chapter, which takes an even deeper dive into the accounting principles such as debits, credits, T-accounts, depreciation, and other items might not be everyone's cup of tea.

That's okay. They're not exactly my own cup of tea.

If, like me, you prefer to hire someone to do your accounting, the next chapter is a great overview of what they're doing and what they're up to. It's a fantastic review of the workings of what an accountant does. And, as always, it's there for you to return to.

So, if you merely skim through it or skip it, I won't judge you. Neither will D.F.

But we wanted to make sure it's there, in order to make this introductory look at accounting for authors more complete.

CHAPTER FIFTEEN:
Deeper Dives!

DFH

Debits, Credits, and "T-Account"

When transactions are recorded in the double-entry method (balancing the seesaw), they're accomplished using **debits** and **credits**. But that does not mean debits are always positive and credits are always negative. It simply means that each double-sided entry will have an equal number of line items so that the overall 'total', if you will, nets to zero.

And whether a debit increases or decreases a general ledger account depending on the *natural state* of that account.

For **asset** and **expense** accounts, a **debit will always** *increase* **the value**.

For **liability, equity, and revenue accounts,** a **debit will always** *decrease* **the value**.

Earlier I showed you a sample Chart of Accounts. Here it is again, only with more columns added so that you can follow along and see which account balances would be raised with a debit versus the ones that would be lowered with a debit. Once you get comfortable with that concept, then it just becomes a question of making sure that when you book your entries, your 'seesaw' is balanced:

G/Lcode	Description	TYPE	DEBITS	CREDITS
11150	Cash-Operating	(1) Asset	Increase	Decrease
11400	Cash-Petty Cash	(1) Asset	Increase	Decrease
12000	Accounts Receivable	(1) Asset	Increase	Decrease
12990	Allowance for Bad Debts	(1) Asset	Increase	Decrease
14110	Inventory	(1) Asset	Increase	Decrease
15704	Capital Expenditures	(1) Asset	Increase	Decrease
15990	Prepaids	(1) Asset	Increase	Decrease
16000	Building	(1) Asset	Increase	Decrease
16100	Computer Equipment	(1) Asset	Increase	Decrease
16200	Leasehold Improvements	(1) Asset	Increase	Decrease
16300	Office Equipment	(1) Asset	Increase	Decrease
16400	Plant Machinery & Equipment	(1) Asset	Increase	Decrease
16500	Transportation Equipment	(1) Asset	Increase	Decrease
16900	Accumulated Depreciation	(1) Asset	Increase	Decrease
18100	Deposits	(1) Asset	Increase	Decrease
18300	Copyright / Trademark	(1) Asset	Increase	Decrease
21000	Accounts Payable	(2) Liability	Decrease	Increase
21300	Sales Tax Payable	(2) Liability	Decrease	Increase
21900	Federal Income Tax Payable	(2) Liability	Decrease	Increase
23400	Accrued Professional & Legal	(2) Liability	Decrease	Increase
24100	Accrued Other	(2) Liability	Decrease	Increase
26000	N/P-Current Portion	(2) Liability	Decrease	Increase
26300	Unearned Income	(2) Liability	Decrease	Increase
27900	N/P - Current (negative from LDT)	(2) Liability	Decrease	Increase
31000	Common Stock	(3) Equity	Decrease	Increase
31300	Retained Earnings	(3) Equity	Decrease	Increase
31400	S Corp Distributions	(3) Equity	Decrease	Increase
41100	Revenue	(4) Income	Decrease	Increase
51100	COGS	(8) Expense	Increase	Decrease
60110	Advertising	(8) Expense	Increase	Decrease
60120	Auto Expense	(8) Expense	Increase	Decrease
60160	Delivery	(8) Expense	Increase	Decrease
60240	Dues & Subscriptions	(8) Expense	Increase	Decrease
60242	Equipment - Rent	(8) Expense	Increase	Decrease
60270	Equipment - Repairs	(8) Expense	Increase	Decrease
60280	Insurance - Property & Casualty	(8) Expense	Increase	Decrease
60286	Insurance - Liability	(8) Expense	Increase	Decrease
60287	Meals & Entertainment	(8) Expense	Increase	Decrease
70100	Bad Debts	(8) Expense	Increase	Decrease
80132	Bank & Card Fees	(8) Expense	Increase	Decrease
80220	Computer/Software	(8) Expense	Increase	Decrease
90110	Interest Expense	(8) Expense	Increase	Decrease
90130	Other Income and Expenses	(8) Expense	Increase	Decrease
90150	Interest Revenue	(8) Expense	Increase	Decrease
90160	Gain (Loss) from Fixed Asset Disposition	(8) Expense	Increase	Decrease
90190	Charitable Contributions	(8) Expense	Increase	Decrease

The way to help make sure your entries (your seesaw) balances is to use a "T-account" visual aid, which looks like this:

For every line item that has a value in the DEBIT column, another line item must have a corresponding value in the CREDIT column, and the totals (showing in the two green boxes) should always match.

Here are some examples of how the T-account thing works:

1) I buy a cover for my new e-book. I spend $75, and I am using the *cash-basis* method.

The entry would be:

GL CODE	DESCRIPTION	Debit	Credit
51100	COGS	75.00	
11150	Cash - Operating		75.00
		75.00	75.00

So, I have INCREASED the value of my COGS account by $75 and I have DECREASED the value of my bank account by $75.

2) I made $250 in sales, but I am using the *accrual-basis* method of accounting, so I am recording those sales when they happen, NOT when I get paid for them:

GL CODE	DESCRIPTION	Debit	Credit
12000	Accounts Receivable	250.00	
41100	Revenue		250.00
		250.00	250.00

Then later, when that $250 gets deposited into my bank account, I will need to 'move' that $250 out of Receivables and over to my bank account, so, I would need to make this additional entry:

GL CODE	DESCRIPTION	Debit	Credit
11150	Cash-Operating	250.00	
12000	Accounts Receivable		250.00
		250.00	250.00

Here's a quick-reference guide to help you remember debits and credits and how they affect the different General Ledger accounts:

```
ASSETS and EXPENSES  Debits make them BIGGER
                      Credits make them SMALLER

LIABILITIES, EQUITY, and INCOME  Debits make them SMALLER
                                  Credits make them BIGGER
```

***

Fixed Assets

When an item is bought, it is important to know what should and should not make the fixed assets section of your bookkeeping process. The question to ask is:

Will this item have a useful life of more than one year?

If the answer is 'yes', you might consider logging it on your books as a fixed asset rather than an expense.

Most businesses set their own dollar threshold as an aid to decide what to expense and what to record as a fixed asset. For a purchase under $500, for example, they may opt to just let that be recorded as an expense and be done with it.

However, the dollar value isn't the determining factor when asking 'should I record this as an asset or not?' The determining factor is the useful life span of that item.

For items costing more than $500 AND having a useful life of longer than a year, listing them as fixed assets and slowly reducing their value over time rather than just taking the hit on your expense section of your Income Statement all at once can come in handy.

For authors, the single best example I can give is buying a new computer. Even though technology is moving at a blistering pace, a computer should have a useful life of more than twelve months.

***

Depreciation

I recommend the *straight-line depreciation method*, which takes the initial price paid, subtracts any salvage value, divides the result by the number of years of 'useful life', then divides that by twelve to get to a monthly depreciation amount.

Example: I buy a brand-new computer for $1,200. I expect to get three years' useful life out of it, and I estimate that in three years' time the salvage value (i.e., what I might be able to get for it if I sell it) will be $200.

Straight-Line Depreciation Formula:
$1200 - $200 = $1000 / 3 = $333.33 per year = $27.78 per month in depreciation.

The Accounting Entries:
To record the purchase:
- Decrease Cash $1200 (credit)
- Increase Fixed Assets $1200 (debit)
- *Then monthly, you would make an entry to:*
- Decrease Fixed Assets $27.78 (credit)
- Increase Depreciation $27.78 (debit)

***

Liabilities — Short-term versus Long-Term

Whether a liability lands in the current or long-term section of your Balance Sheet depends entirely on how soon that liability will be paid off. For items that you expect to be paid in full in *under* twelve months' time, they get booked into the current liabilities section. Long-term liabilities will not be applicable to most authors.

***

Prepaids

Prepaids, as the name suggests, are items you've *paid in advance,* and typically these are things like a lump-sum payment for an annual membership.

Booking those as a prepaid expense means that instead of your Income Statement taking that entire hit at once, you can spread it out (allocate it) across the entire year.

Let's say that I signed up for a marketing service that required a year's payment up front, and the cost was $500. Spreading that out over a year means that each month I need to 'move' $41.66 out of prepaids and over into expenses.

The Accounting Entries:

To record the purchase:

- Decrease Cash $500 (credit)
- Increase Prepaids $500 (debit)
- *Then monthly, I would make an entry to:*
- Decrease Prepaids $41.66 (credit)
- Increase Marketing Expense $41.66 (debit)

***

Inventory

For authors, inventory is simply any physical copies of your work *IF you are using the accrual-basis method.* (Remember: <u>inventory does not exist in the cash-basis method—you would simply expense the items when you buy them and go on with your day.</u>)

BUT if you *are* using the accrual method, and if you ordered paperback copies for a book signing, the value of those books is recorded on your Balance Sheet as inventory (at the <u>price you paid for them</u>, NOT the sales value).

When they are sold, your inventory value goes down (that cost moves OFF your balance sheet and over to your Income Statement as Cost of Goods Sold). If you buy more book stock, your inventory value goes up again.

The Accounting Entries (Accrual-basis method):

To record the purchase:

- Decrease Cash (credit)
- Increase Inventory (debit)

- *Then once books sell:*
- Decrease Inventory (credit)
- Increase Cost of Goods Sold (expenses) (debit)

The Accounting Entries (Cash-basis method):
To record the purchase:
- Decrease Cash (credit)
- Increase Cost of Goods Sold (expenses) (debit)

I've had an author friend ask me previously about 'carryover of inventory'. Basically, if I buy $300 worth of books in 2021 and don't sell them until 2022, they *automatically* carry over <u>in the accrual-basis method</u>; remember I said that unlike the Income Statement accounts, which reset to zero at the end of the financial year, Balance Sheet accounts are *cumulative*. So that 2021 purchase of book stock will remain on my Balance Sheet going into the new year. They won't come out of inventory until I sell them.

Unless I'm using the *cash-basis method*, in which case they would have never landed in Inventory to begin with.

***

Practice Build—Balance Sheet and Income Statement—Accrual Method

Let's try to build out an *accrual-basis* balance sheet and an income statement with the following sample data set:

- Sallie has just finished year one as an indie author.
- Her total sales were $8,281.88 for the year
- She has already paid out $6,242.56 total to get her five books on the market
- She has two bills totaling $308.54 that she has received but not paid yet
- She prepaid a yearly subscription for $201.76
- Sallie also has a book signing event coming up in early February, so she bought $300 worth of paperbacks to take with her.

Remember, if Sallie is using the *accrual method*, she can record everything in real-time, regardless of when she gets paid or makes the payment, and she can also record inventory.

YTD Sales = **$8,281.88**; she has been paid **$7,411.32** so far and is owed another **$870.56**

YTD Expenses = **$6,242.56**

Net Profit/loss = sales – expenses = **$2,039.32**

Accounts Payable = **$308.54**

Prepaid Expenses = **$201.76**

Inventory = **$300**

Balance in her business checking account at year-end is **$975.54**.

Sallie's income statement at the end of the year would look like this:

INPUT YOUR DATA (per month $)		
Income Statement - ACCRUAL BASIS	**FYE Total**	
Month's sales (When EARNED)	$	8,281.88
YTD Gross Income	$	8,281.88
EXPENSES:		
COGS:		
Cover Design	$	911.25
Editing	$	-
Formatting	$	73.50
Barcodes/ISBN's	$	20.00
Book Stock Order	$	-
	$	-
	$	-
	$	-
	$	-
TOTAL COGS	$	1,004.75
G&A:		
Mailchimp - Monthly	$	948.66
Bookfunnel - Monthly	$	180.00
Microsoft - Annual (renews Aug)	$	185.24
ScribeCount - Monthly	$	70.00
Story Origin - Annually	$	74.62
Dues & Subs - ALLi, Patreon	$	195.08
Wordpress - Annual (renews April)	$	337.80
WooComm - Annual (renews Oct)	$	31.39
CPA Fees / PA fees	$	323.20
G SUITE - Annual - (renews Oct)	$	77.94
Promo Spend (from Ad Spend Tab)	$	2,813.88
TOTAL G&A	$	5,237.81
TOTAL EXPENSE	$	6,242.56
Net Income Gain / (Loss)	$	2,039.32

And her balance sheet under the accrual method would look like this:

ASSETS			
Current Assets			
Cash Accounts		$	975.54
Accounts Receivable – Net		$	870.56
Inventory		$	300.00
Prepaid Expenses		$	201.76
Total Current Assets		$	2,347.86
Long–Term Assets			
Fixed Asset Value		$	–
Less Accumulated Depreciation		$	–
Net Fixed Assets		$	–
Other Assets (Deposits, IP, copyright, trademarks, customer lists)			
Deposits		$	–
IP (copyright, trademarks)		$	–
Less Accumulated Amortization of IP		$	–
Net Other Assets		$	–
Total Assets		**$**	**2,347.86**
LIABILITIES AND OWNERS' EQUITY			
Current Liabilities			
Current Portion of Long–Term Debt		$	–
Line of Credit		$	–
Accounts Payable		$	308.54
Accrued Expenses		$	–
Unearned Income		$	–
Total Current Liabilities		$	308.54
Long–Term Debt			
Financial Institutions		$	–
Stockholders		$	–
Less Current Portion of Long–Term Debt		$	–
Net Long–Term Debt		$	–
Owners' Equity			
Common Stock		$	–
Retained Earnings		$	2,039.32
Owner Distributions			
Total Equity		$	2,039.32
Total Liabilties and Owners' Equity		**$**	**2,347.86**

Practice Build—Balance Sheet and Income Statement—Cash Method

Since Sallie cannot record any pending transactions with the cash method, she needs to capture *only what has been funded*, whether outbound (expenses) or inbound (royalty payment). As a result, her year-to-date sales will be a different number, because she must capture all *cash paid to her* within the year:

Jan	Feb	Mar	Apr	May	Jun	Jul	Aug	Sep	Oct	Nov	Dec	FYE Total
Nov 2020 sales	Dec 2020 sales	Jan sales	Feb sales	March sales	April sales	May sales	June sales	July sales	Aug sales	Sept sales	Oct sales	
$ 243.58	$ 1,279.85	$ 1,296.84	$ 513.63	$ 1,944.31	$1,037.61	$ 692.12	$ 401.45	$ 317.60	$ 379.86	$ 431.93	$ 403.97	$ 8,934.75

According to the payments Sallie has received, she had **$8,934.75** in sales.

YTD Expenses = **$6,513.01**

Net Profit/loss = sales – expenses = **$2,421.74**

Accounts Payable, Accounts Receivable and Inventory are all **not applicable** on a cash-basis; any book stock she buys simply gets expensed out.

If she didn't pull any of the profit she made out to do something else with it, her cash account and her retained earnings should match at the end of year one. But the balance in her business checking account only shows $975.54; therefore, the difference of $1,446.20 is shown as an owner distribution on the balance sheet.

Sallie's income statement would look like this:

INPUT YOUR DATA (per month $)		
Income Statement - CASH BASIS	**FYE Total**	
Month's sales (When PAID)	$	8,934.75
YTD Gross Income	$	8,934.75
EXPENSES:		
COGS:		
Cover Design	$	911.25
Editing	$	-
Formatting	$	73.50
Barcodes/ISBN's	$	20.00
Book Stock Order	$	300.00
	$	-
	$	-
	$	-
	$	-
TOTAL COGS	$	1,304.75
G&A:		
Mailchimp - Monthly	$	948.66
Bookfunnel - Monthly	$	180.00
Microsoft - Annual (renews Aug)	$	185.24
ScribeCount - Monthly	$	70.00
Story Origin - Annually	$	74.62
Dues & Subs - ALLi, Patreon	$	165.53
Wordpress - Annual (renews April)	$	337.80
WooComm - Annual (renews Oct)	$	31.39
CPA Fees / PA fees	$	323.20
G SUITE - Annual - (renews Oct)	$	77.94
Promo Spend (from Ad Spend Tab)	$	2,813.88
TOTAL G&A	$	5,208.26
TOTAL EXPENSE	$	6,513.01
Net Income Gain / (Loss)	$	2,421.74

And her Balance Sheet will be much more stream-lined:

BALANCE SHEET		
Month / year		Month / year
ASSETS		
Current Assets		
Cash Accounts	$	975.54
Fixed Assets		
Fixed Asset Value	$	-
Less Accumulated Depreciation	$	-
Net Fixed Assets	$	-
Total Assets	$	975.54
LIABILITIES AND OWNERS' EQUITY		
Current Liabilities		
Unearned Income		
Owners' Equity		
Retained Earnings	$	2,421.74
Owner Distributions	$	(1,446.20)
Total Owner's Equity	$	975.54
Total Liabilties and Owners' Equity	$	975.54

***

In both versions of the Income Statement that we just looked at, the presumption is that Sallie doesn't care to break out her sales and expenses in any way; they were entered as lump sums.

But if you want to track your stuff by format (e-book versus paperback versus audio) or by pen name, or by series or book title, you certainly can. And I highly recommend breaking things out at least a little bit, because structuring your Income Statement to drill down like that can reveal some interesting trends.

To do this, you simply need to make sure that *for every revenue subset, there's a corresponding COGS subset,* like this:

	A	B
Income Statement - CASH BASIS		**Jan**
Month's sales (When EARNED)		Nov prior yr sales
Audiobook	$	125.00
Paperback	$	62.50
E-Book	$	479.00
YTD Gross Income	$	666.50
COGS: Audiobook		
Cover Design	$	50.00
Editing		
Formatting		
Barcodes/ISBN's	$	6.00
Narration		
Translation		
TOTAL AUDIOBOOK COGS	$	56.00
COGS: Paperback		
Cover Design		
Editing		
Formatting	$	100.00
Barcodes/ISBN's	$	6.00
Translation		
Book Stock		
TOTAL PAPERBACK COGS	$	106.00
COGS: E-Book		
Cover Design	$	75.00
Editing		
Formatting		
Barcodes/ISBN's	$	6.00
Translation		
TOTAL E-Book COGS	$	81.00
TOTAL COGS	$	243.00
GROSS PROFIT / (LOSS)	$	423.50

In our example above, the author has a positive *overall* Gross Profit/Loss for January, but when we look more closely at each format, we see this:

Audiobook = $125 in revenue -$56 in costs = $69 profit
Paperback = $62.50 in sales - $106 in costs= ($43.50) loss
E-Book = $479 in sales - $81 in costs = $398 profit

One warning here: Personally, I would *not* structure my Income Statement by retail storefront. The reason for this is simple—I'd have to remember to divide out each COGS line item not only by the number of storefronts, but possibly by the number of sales per storefront, and that to me is just too much work.

Remember that past a certain point, too much drill-down will become unwieldy and harder to navigate—particularly if you are building your reports by hand.

For that reason, I recommend *by format*, as shown here, and capping it at the following categories where applicable:

- Audio
- Paperback—Regular Print
- Paperback—Large Print
- Hardcover
- eBook
- Serialized (i.e., Radish, Kiss, Dreame, etc. if applicable)

If you don't have your books in all these formats, that's fine—just leave out the ones that you do not need.

Note about *Translations*: You may want to list translations of your work as its own revenue and expense areas, or you may opt to roll them into the format(s) listed above; that's totally up to you, just be consistent in your approach.

For those of you who have more than one pen name —you are certainly welcome to build separate Income Statements per pen name. Just remember that *unless you are treating each pen name as a separate business entity*, your indirect (overhead) costs will need to be portioned out accordingly across all Income Statements, and that your Balance Sheet will still need to show ALL activity in a single report.

CHAPTER SIXTEEN:
In Conclusion and Further Resources

We hope you found this book enlightening and helpful for navigating the accounting aspects of your business.

Our goal was to make the topic less overwhelming and frightening and expressed in terms and a style that fellow authors could understand.

Throughout this book we have referred to several helpful resources.

They are listed in the following appendices. Please note that all of these, including other downloadable resources available at:

www.starkpublishing.ca/accounting

In addition, if you're a do-it-yourself type who just needs some Excel spreadsheets to get started, go to:

www.2ofharts.com/welcome-to-accounting-for-authors/

When you sign up, you'll also be notified of upcoming events such as tutorials, podcasts, and more.

D.F. Hart & Mark Leslie Lefebvre
March 2022

ACKNOWLEDGEMENTS

We'd like to extend our sincere thanks to Mitchell Klingher, CPA, who made sure that the information we shared with you was accurate!

A shout out of appreciation to the beta readers for an earlier advanced reader version of this book. Especially, Sarah Bigelow, Valerie Francis, and Erin Wright for their feedback and thoughts.

And last, but certainly not least, a thank you to all of the awesome authors from the **Wide for the Win** Facebook group who took the time to fill out our survey of the things they would like to see included in this book.

APPENDIX A
Quick Reference Guide: Definitions and Formulas

Accounting Equation: Assets = Liabilities + Equity

Accrual-Basis Method: means of recording transactions; items are recorded *when the activity occurs,* regardless of when money changes hands.

Assets: Things your business OWNS

Balance Sheet: the 'show the math' financial report of the "Accounting Equation"

Break-Even Point: Break-Even Units = Total <u>Fixed</u> Costs / (Price per Unit - <u>Variable</u> Cost per Unit)

Cash-Basis Method: means of recording transactions; items are not recorded until money changes hands.

Cost of Sales (COGS): money spent to *make* your product.

Cost-Per-Click: Cost / # of clicks

Cost-Per-Sale: Cost / # of sales

Double-Entry: Each entry in accounting is two-sided (balancing the see-saw).

Equity: What is left over when you subtract everything you OWE from what you OWN

G&A / Overhead Expenses: money spent to run your business and advertise/sell your product.

Gross Income (Gross Profit/Loss): Sales Revenue - Direct Costs

Gross Margin: (Gross Income / Revenue) x 100

Income Statement: the 'show the math' financial report that lists your revenue and all your expenses.

Liabilities: Things your business OWES

Net Income (Net Profit / Loss): Gross Income - Indirect Costs

Net Margin: (Net Income / Revenue) x 100

Net Return: results of activity - initial cost of activity

Payables: Expenses your business owes that have not been paid for yet

Payback Period: initial cost / first year revenue

Readthrough: # of units Book B / # of units Book A

Receivables: Revenue your business is owed that have not been paid to you yet

Return on Investment (ROI): (net return / initial cost) x 100

APPENDIX B
A Note on Vanity & Scam Publishers

Vanity and scam publishers are one of the most significant evils not only facing authors, but actively trying to take advantage of them.

They are predators. And they are damn good at what they do. It's why there are so many of them.

Predators operate within almost every aspect of writing and publishing. Regardless of whether you choose traditional publishing or self-publishing, the water is rife with them.

They prosper and continue to flourish because they prey on the hopes and dreams of writers. They appear to answer the universal desire to "be published" or to "have a publisher." They also offer mostly useless *smoke and mirror* promotional packages that provide the other thing that seems most elusive to most writers—marketing and publicity.

Their business models, which have adapted over the years appears to be all kinds of things—and their marketing efforts are powerful and convincing, even to the most skeptic and savvy authors. But it's mostly made up of one sharp focus.

Taking money from authors.

So the first rule I think that applies is something we discussed in this book, but bears repeating.

Money should flow to the author.

If the money flows from the author to the "publisher," then you're not dealing with a real publisher. You're dealing with a predator.

And these predators are brilliantly creative and deceptive. They are good at masquerading as publishers but need to be seen for the wolves in sheep's clothing that they are.

But if you are familiar with the signs, it's easy to detect predatory publishing companies and service providers. Here are a few things to look out for:

- **Posing as a traditional publisher.** Some vanity publishing outfits will actual call themselves a "real publisher" or refer to themselves as a "traditional publisher." No real publisher ever has to call themselves that or will even refer to vanity publishing because no real publisher ever worries about being seen as a predator. If anywhere on their website they state they aren't a vanity publisher or are a "real publisher," run as fast as you can away from them. I usually adapt Hamlet's "The lady doth protest too much, methinks" perspective and that something more is happening here. Be leery.

- **Promises up front.** Often, on a legitimate publisher's website, there are details about what types of manuscripts they accept, the range of time they are open for submissions, their preferred format, and sometimes expected response rates. Vanity publishers often have few of these requirements, but they are filled with promises of the sales, prestige, and money that will come from publishing with them.

- **Terms such as "co-op" or "partnership" or "hybrid" or "shared costs" or "joint venture."** Use of these terms is typically evidence that the vanity publisher will require money from an author. Remember, their profit comes not from selling books but selling services to authors in order to publish.
- **They reach out to you**. A legitimate publisher will rarely email or call you to offer you a publisher contract out of the blue. Yes, it can happen, and it really does play into our dreams, desires, and somewhat narcissistic belief that we are that "one in a million" author that publishers will be fighting over. But, like those sleazy and pushy companies looking to offer furnace or air-duct cleaning by showing up at your door or calling you out of the blue, there's more in it for them than for you in cold-calling authors.
- **References/Referrals from Agents/Editors**. If an editor, publisher, or agent you submit a manuscript to replies with any sort of "this is excellent, but it just needs some editing work" and then refers you to a service or sister company, or partner or referred partner, or whatever with a fee for that service, you are most likely dealing with a predator. They are very likely either in partnership with or receiving a kickback from the vanity publisher.
- **Avoidance.** Any time you have a reasonable question for one of these vanity publishers and they avoid the question or refuse to give you a clear and concrete answer, they're likely trying to hide something.
- **Distribution and Print on Demand**. The majority of legitimate publishers tend to have relationships with warehouses and bookstores. They most often print

and warehouse books available through wholesale distributors and are easily available for bookstores to order and return. While some legitimate publishers use print on demand (POD) technology, they often have bookstore-favorable terms and existing relationships for books to be easily accessible by and available in bookstores (meaning on bookstore shelves and not just an online listing). One way to determine if a publisher is likely a predator is that they mention where their books will be available. Real publishers don't have to state this. You can also call your local bookstore to see if they have any books from a particular publisher or are able to order any in.

- **Ordering**. Whenever a publisher has details clearly stated on their website, requiring order author copies, it might be evidence that their business model isn't to sell books to readers via bookstores but by selling books to authors directly.
- **Pressure**. A real publisher won't pressure an author into signing a contract. They likely also won't phone an author. They have thousands of other manuscripts sitting in their slush pile. So, any time a "publisher" requires that you reply immediately because this is an offer available only for a limited time, they are playing upon your fears and desire to be accepted and are more than likely counting on that pressure to override your cautious natural logic.

APPENDIX C
Resources Referenced in this Book

Books

Closing the Deal on Your Terms: *Agents, Contracts and Other Considerations*, Kristine Kathryn Rusch, WMG Publishing, 2016.

Estate Planning for Authors: *Your Final Letter (and why you need to write it now)*, M.L. Buchman, Buchman Bookworks, 2017.

Financial Statements, Third Edition: *A Step-by-Step Guide to Understanding and Creating Financial Reports*, Thomas R. Ittelson, Career Press, 2020.

Links (In order of appearance)

Small Business Administration
United States of America:
https://www.sba.gov/business-guide/launch-your-business/choose-business-structure
https://www.sba.gov
Australia: https://asic.gov.au/
Canada: https://www.canada.ca/en/revenue-agency
European Union: https://ec.europa.eu/info/business-economy-euro/doing-business-eu
New Zealand: https://www.business.govt.nz/starting-a-business/

United Kingdom: https://www.gov.uk/topic/company-registration-filing

BookTrakr: https://www.booktrakr.com/
BookReport: https://www.getbookreport.com/
ScribeCount (Affiliate Link):
https://www.scribecount.com/?ref=dfhart

D.F. Hart's Accounting for Authors page:
https://2ofharts.com/welcome-to-accounting-for-authors/

Quickbooks: https://quickbooks.intuit.com/

Master Resources Links: https://starkpublishing.ca/accounting

ABOUT THE AUTHORS

Texas native D.F. Hart always intended to grow up and be a college professor teaching Shakespeare and Chaucer and writing fiction in her off time. Life had other plans and as a result she's been working in accounting for the last twenty-five years. She earned her MBA with Accounting concentration while working full-time.

Although she wrote her first novel in 2010, not much happened until 2018, when the writing bug re-surged with a vengeance, and she went indie.

To date she has seventeen books under her belt using two pen names—D.F. Hart for mystery/thriller stories, and Faith Hart for contemporary romance.

You can learn more about D.F. Hart at www.2ofharts.com

***

Mark's highly successful experience in the publishing and bookselling industry spans more than three decades. He has worked in almost every type of brick and mortar, online and digital bookstore.

The former Director of self-publishing and author relations for Rakuten Kobo, and the founding leader of *Kobo Writing Life*, Kobo's free direct-to-Kobo publishing tool, Mark thrives on innovation, particularly as it relates to digital publishing.

He writes full-time and mentors and coaches authors and publishers about digital publishing opportunities both 1:1 and via his Stark Reflections on Writing & Publishing weekly podcast.

You can learn more about Mark at www.markleslie.ca

Selected Books by the Authors

D. F. Hart's Fiction Titles:
(Thriller/Suspense)

Wall of Secrets (Prequel)

Book of secrets

List of Secrets

Web of Secrets

Path of Secrets

Carnival of Secrets

House of Secrets

End of Secrets – Summer 2022

One Last Gift

An Anthology by James N. Richardson

(D.F. Hart, Editor & Publisher)

D.F. Hart writing as Faith Hart
(Contemporary Romance / Romantic Suspense):

Never Say Sorry

Save Me a Dance

Falling into Place

Love Notes

Read My Lips

Out of the Blue

One Last Try

Saving Brielle – March 2022

Mark Leslie Lefebvre's Books
Books for Writers

Stark Publishing Solutions

The 7 Ps of Publishing Success

Killing It on Kobo

An Author's Guide to Working with Libraries and Bookstores

Wide for the Win

Publishing Pitfalls for Authors

Co-authored titles

Taking the Short Tack: Creating Income and Connecting with Readers using Short Fiction_*(with Matty Dalrymple)*

The Relaxed Author: Take the Pressure off Your Art and Enjoy the Creative Journey_(with Joanna Penn)

Under the name Mark Leslie

Canadian Werewolf Series
This Time Around (Short Story)

A Canadian Werewolf in New York

Stowe Away (Novella)

Fear and Longing in Los Angeles

Fright Nights, Big City

Lover's Moon

Other Novels
Evasion

I, Death

Story Collections
One Hand Screaming

Active Reader

Nocturnal Screams

Nobody's Hero

As Editor

North of Infinity II

Campus Chills

Tesseracts Sixteen: Parnassus Unbound

Fiction River 23: Editors' Choice

Fiction River 25: Feel the Fear

Fiction River 31: Feel the Love

Fiction River 32: Superstitious

Obsessions

Pulphouse #10

Halloween Harvest

Non-Fiction Paranormal / Ghost Stories

Haunted Hamilton

Spooky Sudbury (with Jenny Jelen)

Tomes of Terror

Creepy Capital

Haunted Hospitals (with Rhonda Parrish)

Macabre Montreal (with Shayna Krishnasamy)

Too Macabre for Montreal (with Shayna Krishnasamy)

Lightning Source UK Ltd.
Milton Keynes UK
UKHW021213040822
406846UK00008B/1897